# BUSINESS AND SOCIETY

*By*

Sunita Singh-Sengupta, Ph.D.

*Faculty,*
*Behavioural Sciences Group*
*Indian Institute of Management*
*Calcutta*

DISCOVERY PUBLISHING HOUSE
NEW DELHI-110002

First Published-2003

Reprinted: 2013

ISBN 81-7141-625-X



*Published by*

DISCOVERY PUBLISHING HOUSE

4831/24, Ansari Road, Prahlad Street,
Darya Ganj, New Delhi-110002 (India)
Phone: 3279245 • Fax: 91-11-3253475
E-mail:dphtemp@indiatimes.com

*Printed at:* Dynamic printers, Delhi

# CONTENTS

# PREFACE

Organisations have become the most powerful institutions in contemporary society. They seem to struggle with the question how to maintain the sustainable competitive advantage and keep people 'tied' to the organisation. The trend suggests a growing need for a new direction, for new values, strongly felt among people in and around organisations. Therefore, creating quality is thus no longer limited to the boundaries of the organisation. It implies a focus on the organisation as a whole embedded in society.

In today's volatile environment of business, competitive advantages of firms are temporary, top management do not, and cannot, have all the answers to increasingly complex and rapidly changing problem situations facing their firms. It is argued whether we like it or not, that organisations are the "building blocks" of contemporary society. This implies rethinking, repositioning and revalorizing their role in the context of:

*(a)* how to position the organisation in the society and;

*(b)* how to tap the commitment and potential of the employees.

The present book is an attempt in this direction. The study is manifested through four chapters.

**Chapter—I** presents a review of what has been learnt and where the present investigations might lead.

**Chapter—II** deals with the strategy of the main survey. In this section the details are provided of how, where and when the study was conducted.

Chapter—III presents the findings of the study.

Chapter—IV discusses the results and suggests its implication in the present context.

I take this opportunity to express my heartfelt thanks to Centre for Management Development Studies, Indian Institute of Management Calcutta who provided financial assistance to conduct this project vide their work order no. 019/7-225/ CMDS:SOC:SPPS/1729/98-99.

The warmest appreciation is expressed to all those people and institutions that helped me at one stage or other in making this research a success.

I owe a very special debt of thanks to my respondents who extended their co-operation and participated in the study.

Finally I am deeply indebted to my father late Parmanand Singh who nurtured in me the basic training of hard work and success.

**Sunita Singh-Sengupta**

# Chapter—1
# INTRODUCTION

## Role of Organisations in Society

Organisations have become the most powerful institutions in contemporary society. We no longer have organisations in society but rather a society of organisations. This implies critical examination of their role until now. Today many organisations have come to the conclusion that their present quality systems are no longer "fit for use" and search for ways to integrate, expand or transform what they have been building over the years. The people in and around organisations strongly feel the need for new values and new directions. Creating quality today is no longer purely an issue that stops at the boundaries of the organisation. It implies a focus on the organisations a whole embedded in society (Jonker, 2000).

## Influence of Socio-Cultural Factors on Organisations

Organisations operate in the social milieu and therefore the socio-cultural factors greatly influences it. The people bring these values into the organisations. Despite their imported technologies Indian work organisations are strongly influenced by its socio-cultural factors. There is some evidence that work relationship is not quite contractual. There is strong preference for personalised relationship (Dayal, 1976; Singh-Sengupta, 1990; Sinha, 1980). Excessive dependency seems to be a dominant orientation of the Indian executives (Chattopadhyay, 1975; De, 1974; Sinha, 1970). Weak work values and strong status orientation are found to be pervasive. Agarwal (1976) has attempted to identify the linkages between social and work values. Chattopadhyay and Rao (1970) found that aspirations and worries of industrial workers as well as managers are mostly centered around their self and family. They want to be informed and consulted by their family, because they carry on the familial modes of Indian nurturant superior (Sinha, 1980a). Dayal (1976) has noted that social relationship and organisational performance is not separated in India. Loyalty often gets priority over efficiency. Intrinsic work values are sure to suffer in such a personalised work culture.

***Social values and organisational behaviour:*** Sinha (1980b) has identified some salient features of the Indian social system, which can further exemplify the linkages between social norms and values and organisational behaviour. Indian social institutions and relationships are hierarchically structured where there are meticulously elaborated rules and rituals which are expected to be rigidly conformed to (Kothari, 1970). Hence, Indian tend to arrange themselves in superior-subordinate relationship (Kakar, 1978) which is bound ideally by affective intimacy (Roland, 1980), i.e. *sneh* (affection and care) for the dependents and subordinates and *shradha* (deference) for the superiors. This vertical solidarity (Srinivas quoted by Marriot, 1977) of superior and subordinate is often a part of a social collectivity to which Indians willingly submit. They do not, however, dissolve their individuality or forget their self-interest. The finely differentiated roles and positions within a collectivity allow them to protect and infact enhance their self-interest by developing mutually helpful dyadic cliques within the collectivity. Indians use collectivities for their individual interests. They cultivate linkages with a number of collectivities which are themselves graded into relatively central or peripheral in importance for the individuals compromising them. Indians disposition to grade people into "own" (*apna*) and "others" (*paraya*) reflects a universal phenomenon of categorising persons into in-groups and out-groups. Yet the meticulous extent to which Indian carry this frame (Singh-Sengupta, 1990; Sinha, 1980b) to demarcate social groups and persons within the groups are phenomenal. For "own" and in-group members, Indians are all-sacrificing, loving, affectionate, and loyal. For outsiders, they are callous, manipulative and exploitative. Quite often the only in-group which remains crucial in the minds of Indians is the nuclear family; and the entity which stands distinct, though a lonely, within the family is the "I" of the person. Thus, the gyroscopic "I" and the multiplicity of the social collectivities around the "I" create in Indians a contextual orientation (Roland, 1980) which is quite congruent with their concept of a world which is believed to be fluid (*sansar*). Indians as a result, tend to tolerate ambiguity and differences in views and try to live with the things which are not under their control, and yet manifest manipulativeness and gamesmanship (Ganesh and Malhotra, 1975) which are critical for their survival and prosperity.

***Socio-economic landscape:*** Organisations dominate our socio-economic landscape. Their influence in our everyday lives has grown steady for two centuries (Coleman, 1992), particularly among the wealthiest and most developed regions of the world (Demsetz, 1995). Indeed this "ubiquity of organisations" prompted Herbert Simon (1991) to question the use of the term market economy to describe the structure of our economic interactions (Moran and Ghoshal, 1999). "Would not organisational economy be the more appropriate term"? asks Simon (1991, p. 28). These all suggests that this is the time we should think over the role that the organisations play in economic development, relative to that played by markets.

Organisations in general and firms in particular counterbalance the institutional constraints imposed in markets by muting, replacing, or otherwise modifying market incentives, thereby redefining the motivation for and efficiency of the economic activities they influence. In other words, each firm creates a sharing and combination of resources, including knowledge, in ways that a market cannot. The more plentiful and varied the contexts, the more opportunity individuals have to challenge and to change the forces of development. An organisation that is not adequately enabling and motivating new possibilities is more likely to witness its own decline—a destruction of its own economic structure that will have been induced from within. This manifestation of creative destruction may take decades or even centuries, to materialise, but decline will come as long as someone is better structured to embrace the possibilities that emerge.

If the organisation does remain viable, it will be because its economic structures encourage the institutional changes that would support the creative response. Such structures, whether they exist within a firm or a nation, are likely to be characterised by institutional pluralism.

## Development in Organisations

Over the last century organisations have become the most powerful institutions on earth (e.g., McIntosh et al. 1998; Zadek et al. 1997). There is a dominant conviction that anything—products, behaviour, society and even nature—can be "made". Based on a technical conception of "marketability", man is in control of himself, his behaviour and the natural and social surroundings. Underlying notions such as progress, growth and control have been driving forces leading towards an "enlightened" future for a very long time. Organisations have thus become the "tools" to create comfort, well being, roads, safety and health. This perspective has become so strong that one could call it the "mechanization" of the worldview. History shows that this dominant way of organising creates a self-centered mentality driven by a purely economic paradigm. Being in business first of all means making (financial) profit as if organisations can not be held responsible for what they do. Taking a critical look it appears that through time organisational thinking has only developed within a limited and fractured "reality". The mechanical and technical way of thinking offers seemingly endless variety of paradigms all derived from the same stem. This has resulted in a perspective on organisations that is at its best limited and at worst pathological. The 'natural', human and value-based existence of organisations has either been neglected or lost from sight. Still there is no longer a life "outside" organisations, they have become the 'glue' of society. Still it needs no profound research to discover a publicly widespread scepticism towards organisations (Jonker, 1999).

***Organisation and its identity:*** The social environments in which we exist do not just consist of random assortments or events or actions. There are underlying regularities or patterning in how people behave and in the relationships in which they stand with one another (Jha, 1997). To maintain the sustainable competitive advantage organisations need to develop its identity in the eyes of its stakeholders. Identity involves an entity asking "Who am I"? or in the case of collectivity, "Who are we"? The answer to each single question, however, is often not a single answer. Rather within any single entity there may exist multiple answers and multiple identities. Psychologists and Sociologists, for example, have long argued for the existence of multiple identities within the same individual (Burke, 1937; Feldman, 1979; James, 1890 Markus and Nurius, 1986; McCall and Simmons, 1978; Stryker and Serpe, 1982; Tajfel and Turner, 1979). Mead (1934) suggests that a "Parliament of selves" exist within each person. Organisations can be well understood as individuals and, therefore, have been conceptualized as having many "selves" (Albert and Whetten, 1985; Ashforth and Mael, 1996, Cheney, 1991; Foreman and Whetten, 1997; Golden-Biddle and Rao, 1997; Kramer, 1993; Pratt and Rafaeli, 1997; Reger et al. 1998). These "selves" are manifested by the actions of the organisations. Giddens (1984) distinguishes practical consciousness from discursive consciousness. Those who have only practical consciousness can simply say *what* they do. But those who have discursive consciousness can say not only what they do but *why* and *how* they do so.

Thus an organisational identity should enhance individual self esteem if it is perceived as legitimate—that is, if it is perceived as "desirable, proper, and appropriate within some socially constructed system of norms, values, beliefs and definitions (Suchman, 1995, p. 574).

***Culture and values:*** People's self-concepts reflect internalization of the values, beliefs and meanings from the larger culture in which they (and organisations) are embedded (Erez and Early, 1993). Scott and Lane (2000) suggest that people's perceived overlap with an organisation will enhance their self esteem (i.e., the attractiveness of the overlap) only to the extent they view prototypical characteristics of the organisation as consistent with norms, values, and definitions of the embedding culture.

Culture encompasses patterned ways of thinking (Kluckholm, 1954), mental programs (Hofstede, 1980), and shared meaning systems (Shweder and Levine, 1984). To a large degree, culture provides an interpretive framework through which individuals make sense of their own behaviour, as well as the behaviour of collectivities in their society.

The impact of national culture on the employees work behaviour, specially, in terms of work related values were intensely examined by Geert Hofstede (1980, 1991) who suggested four dimensions to interpret behaviour at workplace in one's socio-cultural context. These dimensions were:

*(1)* ***Power distance:*** measures human inequality in organisations looking at the boss's decision-making style, employees' fear of disagreeing with the superior, and how subordinates prefer a boss to make decisions. Essentially, it looks at how less powerful people validate the power structure. Cultures with a low score tend to respect individuals, strive for equality and value happiness;

*(2)* ***Uncertainty avoidance:*** explains each society's search for the truth and the anxiety people fell in a situation with conflicting values or unstructured outcomes. Cultures with high uncertainty avoidance try to minimise the anxiety with a thorough set of strict laws and behaviour norms. Low uncertainty avoidance cultures tend to have fewer rules and more acceptance of diversity of thought and behaviour;

*(3)* ***Individualism:*** looks at the degree to which people are parts of groups or on their own. In collective societies, everyone is born into a strong clan of uncles, aunts and cousins (even third and fourth) who are part of one unit. Each person contributes to the group and at some time receives care from the group. Loyalties are to the group above everything else. In more individualistic societies, people are more or less on their own and are expected to take care of themselves and their immediate family;

(4) ***Masculinity:*** versus its opposite, femininity examines how roles are distributed between sexes. The predominant pattern of socialization worldwide is for men to be more assertive and women to be more nurturing.

*Credos of the organisation.* The extensive research carried out by Collins and Porras (Palazzi and Starcher (2001) found evidence in nearly all of the visionary companies of a credo or a core ideology that existed not only as words but as a vital shaping force. These credos defined the core values and a sense of purpose well beyond just making money. They study showed that the visionary companies have generally been more ideologically driven and less profit-driven as compared to those, which were rated to be not so successful. Whether in the form of mission statement, code of conduct, or credo, the authenticity and consistent alignment with the ideology is more important than the specific content.

## Sustainable Competitive Advantage

The fundamental basis of long-run success of a firm is the achievement and maintenance of a sustainable competitive advantage. The idea of a sustainable competitive emerged in 1984, when Day suggested types of strategies that may help to "sustain the competitive advantage" (p. 32). The actual term "Sustainable Competitive Advantage" emanated in 1985, when Porter discussed the basic types of competitive strategies that a firm can possess (low-cost or differentiation) in order to achieve a long-run SCA. Interestingly, Porter presented no formal conceptual definition in his discussion. Barney (1991) has probably come the closest to a formal definition by offering the following: "A Firm is said to have a sustained competitive advantage when it is implementing a value creating strategy not simultaneously being implemented by any current or potential competitors and when these other firms are unable to duplicate the benefits of this strategy (p. 102).

In order to offer a formal conceptual definition of the term, it may be helpful to consider the meaning and implications of all three terms. Webster's Dictionary defines the term "advantage" as the superiority of position or condition, or a benefit resulting from some course of action. "Competitive" is defined in Webster's as relating to, characterised by, or based on competition (rivalry). Finally, Webster's shows the term "sustain" to mean to keep up or prolong.

The next step in crafting a formal conceptual definition of SCA is to consider these dictionary definitions in a business-specific context. Based on the definition of "competitive" presented above, SCA should be viewed by a firm from an external perspective. Competition is based on rivalry between two or more parties; thus, the focus of SCA should be how long a firm can keep competitors at bay. A firm who approaches the achievement of SCA from an internal perspective is missing the point. A particular strategy based on firm resources irrespective of what competitors are doing certainly could be sustained. However, it is the external focus—the focus on competitors—that allows a firm to recognize and/or create unique resources. This uniqueness is what gives a firm the advantage. The advantage (or superiority) is sustained (or prolonged) as long as the unique strategy provides added value to customers, and as long as competitors cannot find a way to duplicate it.

In today's volatile environment of business, competitive advantages of firms are temporary, top management do not, and cannot, have all the answers to increasingly complex and rapidly changing problem situations facing their firms. It is argued whether we like it not, that organisations are the "building blocks" of contemporary society. This implies rethinking, repositioning and revalorizing their role in the context of:

1. Positioning of the organisation in the society and
2. Tapping the commitment of the employees

## Positioning of the Organisation in the Society

In every organisation two types of cultures prevail: (a) professional culture and (b) community culture. The strength of a company including both its creativity and organisational flexibility depends consequently both on its professional competence and social competence of its employees. The quality of a company's community culture appears to have a decisive influence on its professional creativity. Cultural knowledge also unites the company and its professional culture with the rest of the world local, national, international. Thus, the cultural foundations of professional competence make the employees aware of the variety of relationships in which a company stands to its environment. Consequently, it also makes the company more aware of its moral responsibilities towards nature and community at large. On the basis of strong community culture, the overall purpose of a community can no longer be profit (or maximum profit), but to serve the community.

To position itself in the society the organisations need to be externally focussed. This offers two benefits to the company:

(*a*) It helps the company to understand better the environment it operates in and the needs and concerns of all the parties it has to deal with, be they customers, suppliers, public agents or employees;

(*b*) It demonstrates the inclusiveness of the company within the society it operates in thus generating goodwill among customers and others in society and reinforces the company's reputation.

## Social Responsibility of Organisations

***An organisation is a creation of Society:*** It gets its resources from Society. The society accepts and consumes its outputs. Without the specific sanction of Society, no organisation can prosper. Organisations are citizens (members) of society and as citizens, they owe certain responsibilities to the society. The primary responsibility is to ensure that it does not cause it any damage and the second responsibility is to contribute to its progress.

***Organisations are sub-systems of society:*** They cannot function and remain healthy except when the bigger system remains healthy, just as organs of a body cannot function effectively when the body as a whole, is not healthy. The health of the society is therefore a necessary concern of organisations. The concern can not be one of passive observer. It has to contribute actively to the enhancement of the overall health of the society.

***Corporate social responsibility:*** Business organisations of today are much bigger than in the past and the impact of their operations on society much wider. They have much greater potential to do much greater damage than ever before, through thoughtless actions, if they do not focus on the long-term consequences. Considerations of patronage may blind them to excesses. There is need to consciously transcend the limited interests of a corporation and glorify its causes in terms of the greater good.

Davis (1973) conceived of corporate social responsibility as the obligations of firms to work for social betterment and to achieve social benefits along with economic gains. These obligations are perceived to arise because the corporation is seen to be a citizen in a complex, interdependent world, and is seen to have a responsibility for the good of the larger society that has given it birth and sustained and nurtured it with supportive infrastructure, institutions, resources and facilities (Aram, 1989; Preston and Post, 1975). In addition, the corporation is an institution of vast power and very little accountability (Berle and Means, 1934; Galbraih, 1972), and inculcating corporate social responsibility is a way of bridging this gap.

## Business and Society

Business is a socio-cultural activity, which impacts the lives of many more people than actually involved in the work, or directly benefit from the profits and share dividends of the company. The business need to redefine the way in which a company sees itself, away from a rigid adherence to a narrowly focussed 'single' bottom line, with companies seeing themselves as responsible only to their shareholders, towards a more socially, ethically and environmentally aware definition of themselves as a company 'doing business in the public eye'.

## Business-Social Partnership

Companies that make investments in the social and physical environment today will be the leaders in their business tomorrow. The organisations in its pursuit of social responsibility should redesign itself in order to meet the corporate obligation to the social and economic wellbeing of the community. Every community has a special continuing responsibility towards the people of the area in which it is located. The company should spare its engineers, doctors, and managers, advise the people of the villages and supervise new development undertaken as a cooperative effort by them and the company.

The corporate sector's approach to community development generally does not seem to be a thought-out-strategy but a haphazard effort to get to the maximum mileage with the investing public. Therefore, most of the companies were contended with donating money, something that didn't need too much involvement. For them anything that entailed continuous involvement and responsibility was tedious (Meera Seth, 1998).

For most companies, monetary donation is the most common means of corporate involvement because social development is not the core competence of a company. A Company cannot, therefore, take the role of governmental agencies, but it certainly can supplement the efforts made by the governmental as well as non-governmental organisations. If a company wants to avail the advantages of being socially responsible it seems to have two choices—either hire social development professionals or partner an NGO. The latter option is less explored one but has many advantages, once a good partner is found (Venkateswaran, 1998). The advantages of *partnership mode* is that NGOs provide an entry into the community as social work is their forte. However, there are certain disadvantages of which the companies should be guarded against. Some of the most obvious disadvantages seem—different perceptions on what needs to be done for a community/area and less control on how money is spent.

This gives room to first option *Do-it-yourself mode*. The advantages of this option are that it ensures that development work is in tune with company objectives. It also enables to have better control over the utilization of money. But most of the companies lack skills in social work and have the impression that community keeps expecting more. Therefore, they have restricted themselves to manage their corporate social responsibility through donations. However, money cannot substitute the managerial, technical and marketing skills that companies have. Further such companies are unlikely to reap the benefits of developing a more in-depth relationship with their local communities that may be of strategic and long-term importance to their business (Mehta, 1998).

Local cultures affect how consumers expect companies to behave, as does the response and type of product that a company will sell in a given country. A very good example is Tata Iron and Steel Rural Development Society (TSRDS) established by Tata in the late 1970s. It functions as an NGO, whose purpose is to focus on education and literacy, health and medical activities; agriculture and irrigation, drinking water, vocational training etc. Another example is KGVK (Krishi Gram Vikas Kendra) by Usha Martin. KGVK have not confined itself to a small area close to the factory premises of Usha Martin. As a result it was able to survive on its own, creating a separate identity independent, of the corporate identity prevented KGVK from relying excessively on its corporate parent for funds. A human base for the consideration of problems was encouraged, so that those involved with the project moved beyond input-output ratios and cost-benefit analyses as a justification for the actions. By being removed from the corporate influence, it was possible to shift the non-profit motive from the profit motive.

## Organisational Citizenship and Ethical Work Climate

The emergence of corporate citizenship as a well-accepted managerial practice is closely linked to the growing belief that acting as an exemplary organisation is good business (Burke and Logdson, 1996; Mullen, 1997). Like individuals, organisations too can rise above their bread and butter concerns. They may be able to do so in several different ways. For example, they may extend their accountability beyond their owners or managers to other stakeholders like employees, customers, suppliers, financiers, government, community, etc. That is, they can adopt the view that their survival and well-being depends upon the cooperation of these other stakeholders and in return they must reciprocate by looking after the interests of these stakeholders. A bolder, more ambitious exaltation route is corporate social responsibility, the notion that not only does the organisation have an obligation to look after the interests of its specific stakeholders, it has various obligations to society-at-large in which it operates. A special, more focussed form of corporate social responsibility is the commitment of the organisation to help the domain it operates in to grow and develop. This commitment is particularly relevant in developing societies in which major efforts need to be made in each domain to overcome backwardness and stasis so that a vibrant, self-reliant, innovative, modern society emerges. Yet, past research has failed to establish the existence of a positive association between socially responsible corporate behaviour and business performance (Preston and O'Bannon, 1978; Stanwick and Stanwick, 1998). Nonetheless, given the globalization of business activities, more and more organisations need to gain hindsight into the nature and desirability of corporate citizenship. Corporate Citizenship can be defined, "... as the extent to which businesses meet the economic, legal, ethical and discretionary responsibilities imposed on them by their shareholders" (Maignan, 2000, p. 284).

Creating culture by doing business in public is, therefore, a powerful catalyst for establishing a sustainable society, where everyone is recognized as a legitimate stakeholder able to comment openly. Such openness is therefore, a public conversation that takes place as a part of a public culture and this lies at the heart of corporate citizenship, because it is participation in this public conversation which defines public culture as expressive citizenship (Birch, 2000).

In pursuit of social responsibility the organisation should strive to exemplify the highest standards of business ethics and personal integrity, and would recognize the corporate obligation to the social and economic wellbeing of our community as well as the wellbeing of the employees for bringing them together and mobilizing their collective efforts. The task of making an organisation's strategy socially responsible means, (1) conducting organisational activities within the bounds of what is considered ethical and in general public interest, (2) responding positively to emerging societal priorities and expectations, (3) demonstrating a willingness to take action ahead of regulatory confrontation, (4) balancing stockholder interests against the larger interests of society as a whole, and (5) being a good citizen in the community.

## Social Responsibility: A Strategic Business Investment

The responsibility to society is different from the responsibility it has towards select segments of society like shareholders, customers, employees, dealers, suppliers, Government, etc., all of whom are stakeholders in one form or other. These stakeholders benefit because they directly contribute towards the activities and success of the organisation. The activities however, have impact on persons other than the stakeholders. For example, if a factory allows toxic affluent to pollute the atmosphere or waters, the adverse consequences may or may affect the stakeholders, but will affect many others. The life styles of people living out of the waters, through fishing or ferrying will be affected on a long-term basis. The effect will be on the health of the people, their productive capacities and the economy of the society, lasting perhaps, for generations.

Carroll (1979) thought of corporate social responsibility as consisting of various obligations. The economic obligations of the corporation in market economies extend to being productive and profitable and to meet the needs of customers; the legal obligations are to do business within the limits of the law; the ethical obligations relate to incorporating the codes, norms, and values of society in its business; and the philanthropic or discretionary obligations relate to contributing to social causes (Carroll, 1979). This is a far more comprehensive conception of corporate social responsibility than Friedman's dictum (1970) that the only corporate social responsibility of business in a competitive market economy is to maximise profits (within the limits prescribed by the law).

As against an idealised conception of corporate social responsibility, there have been attempts to determine what business leaders in fact see is the corporate social responsibility of business. In a study of 203 US collegiate business deans and 116 CEOs there was much agreement with such statements as 'responsible corporate behaviour can be in the best economic interest of the stakeholders', 'efficient production of goods and services are no longer the only thing society expects from business', 'long run success of business depends on its ability to understand that it is part of a larger society and to behave accordingly', 'involvement by business in improving its community's quality of life will also improve long run profitability', 'a business that wishes to capture a favourable public image will have to show that it is socially responsible', and 'social problems such as pollution control sometimes can be solved in ways that produce profits from the problem solution' (Ford and McLaughlin, 1984). The agreement was low with statements such as 'since businesses have such a substantial amount of society's managerial and financial resources, they should be expected to solve social problems' and 'other social institutions have failed in solving social problems so business should try'. There was some disagreement as between the CEOs and deans on the idea of social responsibility is needed to balance corporate power and discourage irresponsible behaviour'. The pattern of agreements and disagreements suggests that the business establishment in the US favours that form of corporate social responsibility that is in the best long term interests of business or offers opportunities for profits, but not the one that stems from purely ethical or moral compulsions or social necessity. Both the CEOs and the deans agreed that the American business community's support for socially responsible activities has risen over the past and is likely to rise further in the future.

Since the business establishment in capitalist societies is likely to favour forms of corporate social responsibility that are in the enlightened self-interest of business, the issue whether socially responsive behaviours indeed are associated with corporate financial performance has significant practical consequences. A strong positive relationship should reinforce socially responsible behaviour, a strong negative relationship should discourage it. Extant US research does not suggest any strong relationship between the two (Aupperle, Carroll, and Hatfield, 1985; McGuire, Sundgren, and Schneeweis, 1988). In a study of 241 CEOs of companies listed in Forbes 1981 Annual Directory and their responsiveness vis-a-vis economic, legal, ethical, and philanthropic aspects of corporate social responsibility, no significant relationship was found between a measure of profitability (with and without adjustment for risk) and any of the measures of corporate social responsiveness (Aupperle et. al, 1985). Interestingly, concern for society (consisting of items of legal, ethical, and philanthropic responsibility) was strongly negatively correlated with the economic dimension of social responsibility. Also, in a forced choice 10-point allocation for the four dimensions format, the mean score of the economic dimension of corporate social responsibility at 3.5 was the highest that of the legal dimension was the second highest at 2.5, that of the ethical dimension at 2.2 was the third highest, and that of the discretionary or philanthropic dimension was the lowest at 1.3. Thus, socially productive profit maximization that is consistent with the law may be the predominant definition of social responsibility in corporate America.

Thus, corporate social responsibility may be a consequence rather than an antecedence of corporate financial performance. Fast track, profitable, low risk firms especially may gravitate eventually towards corporate social responsibility. Corporate social responsibility postures in the US may well be substantially image building exercises financed by organisational slack (Cyert and March, 1963; Kraft and Hage. 1989). Interestingly, there is some research evidence from Fortune 500 companies that large firms operating in dynamic, munificent environments are more likely to behave illegally than firms with poor performance (Baucus and Near, 1991). Thus, organisational slack prompts socially responsible behaviour, but is itself some limes a result of unlawful behaviour. Plunder first and get social legitimacy next may be a pattern of behaviour with some of these high slack companies.

A refinement and concretisation of corporate social responsibility may be corporate social performance. Corporate social performance stresses actions and outcomes. Thus corporate social performance is a configuration of principles of social responsibility, processes of social responsiveness, and policies, programmes, and observable outcomes as they relate to the firm's societal relationship (Wartick and Cochran, 1985; Wood, 1991). Wood's corporate social performance model encompasses principles of corporate social responsibility, processes of corporate social responsiveness, and outcomes of corporate behaviour at the institutional (business as a whole), organisational, and managerial levels. For example, at the institutional level the principle enunciated by Davis (1973) is that of legitimacy business must avoid abusing its power. At the organisational level this institutional principle implies the principle of public responsibility for example, an organisation must take responsibility for the negative extrenalities (e.g. pollution, waste) it creates. At the managerial level this public responsibility could be discharged by the use of the manager's discretionary authority to ensure socially responsible outcomes through specific actions and performances. Various processes of corporate social responsiveness can be harnessed, such as environmental assessment, stakeholder management, and issues management, and several outcomes can be expected, including social impacts, social programmes, and social policies. This sort of conceptualization can lead to the development of corporate social policies, such as produce only ecologically sound products, use low polluting technologies, cut costs with recycling, undertake product or process innovations that comply with regulatory requirements, target information on the use of ecologically sound products to specific markets, and choose charitable investments that actually pay off in solving social problems.

## Stakeholder Orientation

One influential stream of thinking on corporate management has stressed that the only stakeholder in a corporation is the owner (Friedman, 1970), the rest being "factors of production" that are agents of the owner. Since agents pursuing their self-interest may not necessarily act in the best interests of the owner, various control mechanisms (such as hierarchies, MIS) and contracts (such as performance based incentive contracts) must be resorted to in order to ensure that corporate behaviour is profit maximizing behaviour. The ethical foundation of all this effort at ensuring profit maximization is the inference of neo—classical economic theory that the only principle that maximizes customer welfare and ensures equity in payments to factors of production in a competitive market economy is the single-minded pursuit of profit maximization (subject to compliance with legal requirements) (Friedman, 1970). However, when markets are imperfect (this is the rule around the world rather than the exception), there are gross inequalities, and large negative externalities of corporate actions, profit maximization as a principle can degenerate into an opportunistic get-rich-fast mindset that does not, either in the short run or in the long run, necessarily lead to Pareto optimality.

As against the logic of profit maximization for maximizing the wealth of the owners of the enterprise is the notion of multiple corporate stakeholders. A stakeholder is an identifiable group or individual who can affect the achievement of an organisation's objectives or who is affected by the achievement of an organisation's objectives—more narrowly a stakeholder is an individual or a group on which the organisation is dependent for its continued survival (Freeman and Reed, 1983, p. 91) Freeman (1984) described the possible impacts of the firm's relationship with a number of stakeholders. Thus, if such stakeholders as suppliers, employees, customers, or the government have positive relations with the organisation, the latter can achieve its objectives more fully and with greater ease. If the relations with any stakeholder are negative they can endanger goal attainment by the organisation, sometimes its survival itself.

Proponents of stakeholder theory have argued that recognising the multiple constituencies that have stakes in the organisation and taking steps to manage the interface with each stakeholder increases the competitive advantage of the organisation (Jones, 1995). The use of the principles of trust, trustworthiness, and cooperativeness in dealing with stakeholders can lower operating costs. Short-term profit maximization amounts to opportunism, and thus has high costs in terms of top heavy control structures, large transactions costs, and poor cooperation in teams in situations where no one member's contribution can be accurately measured and therefore differentially rewarded. Emphasis on corporate morality, the ethic of trust and cooperation, even if it results in some abuses, can strengthen relations with stakeholders and thereby reduce drastically the costs of profit maximizing opportunism. In this form stakeholder theory amounts to enlightened long-term self-interest.

Effective stakeholder management has incorporated ideas of effective management from several management disciplines (Freeman and Reed, 1983). One is participation of stakeholder's in organisational decision making (Dill, 1975), including of adversarial groups such as Nader's Raiders. Another is the application of market orientation to stakeholders understand the needs of each stakeholder and design programmes, services, and products that fulfil these needs. From political science comes the idea of understanding the political nature of the relationship with and between stakeholders by applying such tools as coalitional analysis, conflict management, and unilateralism. From economics comes the idea of allocating organisational resources in relation to the degree of importance of the stakeholders' claims upon the organisation. The involvement of stakeholders in corporate governance is likely to make the latter more democratic, since forums need to be created, such as stakeholder councils, to give representation to stakeholders' interests and suggestions. The corporate board in particular may need to be restructured to reflect stakeholders' concerns and harness their cooperation.

Stakeholder theory incorporates a useful sort of wisdom about how to manage an organisation in its long-term interest. It is when the organisation's management transcends the idea of self-interest and considers meeting the needs of stakeholders as ends in themselves that the first step towards greatness may be taken. It is then that the path becomes thorny, for the question becomes not only how to reconcile the interests of various stakeholders but also how to reconcile their interests with the more narrowly defined interests of the organisation and this requires courage.

*The ethical aspect of social responsibility* has also been put forward in some codes of ethics by business associations in a number of the countries. For example, in Philippines business world witnessed increasing interest in social responsibility among employers and managers as indicated through participation of more than 900 chief executives in the workshops organised by the Bishops Businessmen's Conference for Human Development (BBC) which resulted in a code of ethics for business known as the BBC code of ethics. A survey conducted among over 4000 businesses in the Philippines found that around 70% of those who replied had adopted some form of code of ethics. In Thailand the Buddhist tradition of "sharing happiness and sorrows with others" creates a form of social responsibility among people. Thus, a growing number of business leaders view corporate social investment as an attempt to find a new way to arrange the economic order and improve the benefits of the economic growth (Hopkins, 1999).

One of the dimensions of corporate citizenship is an ethical work climate that includes values, traditions, and pressures exerted in the work environment to make legal and ethical decisions. An ethical climate involves formal values and compliance requirements as well as an understanding of how interpersonal relationships affect the informal interpretation of ethics. Loe (1996) examined the association between an ethical climate and improved organisational processes. When clear barriers are established to limit the opportunity for unethical activities, and when ethical behaviours are rewarded, an ethical climate prevails in an organisation. In an ethical work climate, employees are able to identify ethical issues as they arise and are aware of the company resources available to help them act ethically and according to organisational policy and culture. An ethical climate characterizes businesses that are committed to ethical citizenship.

It may be useful to briefly consider the negative outcomes that may arise from a work climate that does not emphasize ethical conduct before we discuss the benefits of an ethical work climate. The case of Bausch and Lomb is a good illustration. A few years ago, the company's organisational culture was described by Business Week as "A train wreck waiting to happen" (A Blind Ambition @1995, p.80). The company's operations were governed almost exclusively by strict sales and earnings objectives. Under stringent bottom-line pressures and with no counterbalancing values helping them to differentiate right from wrong, managers engaged in unscrupulous pricing and fraudulent billing. These practices translated into a series of lawsuits from customers and distributors, bad publicity, and a sharp decline in the firm's market value.

Thus, a major benefit of an ethical climate is avoidance of negative consequences that may result from unscrupulous conduct in the workplace. Leo's (1996) study suggests that concrete business benefits can be expected from an ethical climate. He conducted a before and after a research design was developed whereby employees assessed the ethical climate of their organisation before and after implementation of an extensive ethics training programme. The intra-firm trust, employee commitment to quality, and market orientation as perceived by organisational members were also rated at the two stages of the research. The findings of this research indicated that, employees who work in an ethical climate are likely to believe that they have to treat all their business partners respectfully, regardless of whether they operate inside or outside of the organisation. As a result, it becomes essential for them to offer the best possible value to all customers. The findings imply that an ethical work climate is likely to have a positive effect on the bottom line, because employees' commitment to quality has been shown to have a positive effect on the firm's competitive position. The findings get support by the study conducted by Heskett, Sasser, and Schlesinger (1997) who found that improved employee commitment to quality is associated with greater customer satisfaction. This is because customer satisfaction is affected directly by customer's perception of customer service (Hartline and Ferrell 1996). In addition, elements of quality, such as service quality, influence the company's image as well as its ability to attract new customers and charge premium prices (Blumberg 1987; Blume 1988; Sonnenberg 1989). Other benefits of employee commitment to quality include greater market share (Kordupleski, Rust, and Zahork 1993; Phillips, Chang and Buzzell 1983; Zeithaml, Berry, and Parasuraman 1988), increased profitability and lower costs (Jacobson and Aaker 1987; Shapiro 1983; Zeithaml, Berry, and Parasuraman 1988), and return on investment (Phillips, Chang, and Buzzell 1983).

In Indian context, WIPRO is a very good example ethical practices and sustaining competitive advantage. WIPRO's strength lies in the fact that it has continuously adapted to change. Integrity and ethics are the cornerstone of the work culture at WIPRO (Venkat Ramani, http:/www.lifepositive.com/mind/ethics and values/ethics—article.html)

## Ethical Approach to Strategic Management

1. ***Stakeholder theory, strategy and ethics:*** Stakeholder theory stems from the suggestion that business should be regarded

as an activity of society, and hence business has responsibilities to a much wider range of stakeholders than merely its shareholders, directors and creditors. It, therefore, concerns who should have what level of say in strategic issues within a company. Hence, it challenges the traditional belief in manager's right to manage and raises questions about responsibility and accountability. Stakeholder theory is also an attempt to avoid a "bolt-on" ethics mentality. This stems from the very persistent basic picture of self-understanding that the business community has about itself, which is the organisation doing its best to "survive" in a 'hostile environment' (Davies, 1992, pp. 1-40). Ethical strategy then becomes some kind of bolt-on-veneer forced upon business by various stakeholders. An alternative way of looking ethics, strategy and stakeholders is to view business as having a pro-active role in creating an ethical society (Goyder, 1993).

2. ***Loyalty and the psychological contract:*** Strategic change often breaches what is known as the "psychological contract". This is implicit in the relationship between every employer and employee, and is often couched in terms of loyalty. An employee will have built-up certain expectations about how they will be treated (based on personal relationships with organisational members). They are then prepared to make sacrifices for "the organisation" in return.

3. ***Responsible decision-making: Rights and responsibilities:*** The nature of decision-making rights and responsibilities affects the ethical sensitivities and behaviour of workers. For example, compensation practices and performance evaluation processes may create incentives or pressures for workers to behave unethically. The corporate norms, values and culture play an important role in promoting or discouraging ethical conduct (Chen et al. 1997; Trevino et al. 1998; Victor and Cullen, 1988). Culture is an important factor affecting the ethical conduct of workers because it can help solve the commitment problem inherent in the structural aspects of organisations (Kreps, 1990). Managers commit to treat and pay their workers fairly, for instance, and if their commitment is credible, workers will respond by trusting management and by making ethical decisions,

the effect of which is increased commitment by management and corresponding ethical actions by workers (James, Jr. 2000). Such ethical decisions improve the organisational climate as it manifests the credos of the organisation in every-day activities. Arrow (1974) and Stone (1975) noted that ethical controls are necessary because the legal system and markets do not necessarily lead to organisational behaviour that takes into consideration moral impacts of business decisions. Responsible decision making behaviour helps in establishing business as a profession and, therefore, can be viewed as attempts to institutionalize the values and the guiding principles of the company in such a way that they become part of the corporate culture and help to socialize new individuals into the culture.

## Linking Strategy with Ethics

Every strategic action a company takes should be ethical because every business has an ethical duty to each of five constituencies: Employees, shareholders, customers, suppliers, and the community at large. Each of these constituencies affects the organisation and is affected by it.

1. *Employees:* We spend a large percentage of our waking hours at work. Our work experience strongly shapes our identities, our sense of self-worth, and the extent to which we can contribute to community life. The quality of life in the workplace and on the job affects our whole life as well as that of our families.

Socially responsible businesses are doing more to provide work which is meaningful and which helps employees develop and realize their potential. They are seeking to provide fair wages, a healthy and safe work environment, and a climate of respect. Management practices and human resource policies often include empowerment of middle management and employees; better information throughout the company; better balance between work, family, and leisure; greater work force diversity; continual education and training; and concern for employability as well as job security. Companies are also finding that profit sharing and share ownership can enhance motivation and productivity and decrease employee turnover.

There is increasing evidence that those practices which provide more meaningful work and higher quality of life in the workplace have a very direct impact on profits through increased productivity, greater innovation, higher quality and reliability, and more skillful and committed people at all levels. Furthermore, many companies find that caring for employees results in greater customer satisfaction. One survey in the United Kingdom concluded that employee loyalty contributes to customer loyalty. Several studies have examined the relationship between good human resource policies and practices and financial performance. One of the most interesting is a study by the PIMS Group (Profit Impact of Market Strategy). Over the years, this group has gathered data on 3,000 "strategic business units", half of which are in Europe. These units were divided into those considered good or poor in the management of their human resources. The criteria used included the following; feeling of belonging, equitable compensation, absence of conflict, sense of accomplishment, participation in decisions, sharing of information, and willingness to change. The comparison of the financial results of these two groups—those rated high on management of human resources and those rated low was quite revealing. For those enterprises operating in complex and turbulent environments, the difference in return on investment of good practices was 16.7% a difference which is enormous by any standard. It was also interesting that the difference was much less significant (+3.5%) for companies in stable environments. But with increasing globalisation, privatisation and deregulation, stable environments are disappearing.

Another study of high performance work practices was based upon a survey of 700 publicly held corporations (in the United States). The practices covered included personnel selection, job design, information sharing, performance appraisal, promotion systems, attitude assessment, incentive systems, and labour-management participation. The upper quartile of firms— those using the best practices—had a return on capital of 11%,—more than twice as high as the remaining firms. The California Public Employees Retirement System (CalPERS) decided recently to take workplace practices into consideration in investing its $ 108 billion pension fund. Their experience has shown that companies which have pushed responsibility down the line, flattened hierarchies, empowered front line workers to make decisions, trained and educated them, shared information, and treated employees as partners trade at a premium on the stock market. Over the five year period 1990 to 1994, these companies outperformed the S&P 500 by about 16 per cent, or about 3 per cent on an annual basis. Profit sharing is an increasingly widespread practice. The popularity of profit sharing varies widely around the globe, varying from 6 to 27% of workers in the developed countries. France, where one in four workers benefit from profit sharing, leads in worker participation since firms with 50 or more employees must, by law, share some of the profits with workers through a deferred profit sharing plan. In most other OECD countries including the United States and Japan, only one in eight workers benefit from profit sharing. Many economists cite three major benefit: it increases productivity, it stabilizes employment by making wages more flexible, and it may raise the total level of employment to the extent that it reduces the marginal cost of taking on one additional worker. An OECD study, which draws on the conclusions of nineteen different studies in France, Germany, Italy, United Kingdom and the United States, concludes that sharing profits significantly increases productivity. Surveys of employers report that employees benefiting from such plans are more receptive to change. The other potential benefits cited above may be real, but are less conclusively supported. In the Bahá'í Writings, profit sharing is strongly encouraged to improve worker motivation and employer worker relations and to make compensation more just.

There are innumerable examples of what companies are doing to improve the quality of life in the workplace. One member of the European Bahá'í Business Forum runs a chain of hotels in the United States and recently placed all managers, including himself, and employees through an intensive training programme to enhance teamwork through better understanding of cultural diversity among employees. Following this, a profit sharing plan was introduced together with an educational campaign to teach employees how to read and understand financial statements. He asserts that these efforts have fostered greater collaboration among employees, enhanced the quality of life in the workplace, and increased the profitability of his hotels.

Another member of EBBF was responsible for developing a large $1 billion greenfield (that is, a brand new industrial site) multi-product site with a series of plants for his company in northern Spain. He designed high performance work systems around autonomous teams, little hierarchy in the structure, wide use of consultative decision making, no job titles or perks for managers, open office arrangement, and a share ownership plan for all employees and managers. Today the plant is said to have the highest productivity and the lowest turnover and absenteeism of any of the eighteen plants of this group in Europe. With women such an important factor in the workplace today, companies are increasingly adopting programmes and policies to make work and the workplace more family-friendly. Companies are providing or helping employees to find day care centres and kindergartens. More generous parental leave policies are being developed, in addition to these policies and practices, some leading companies are finding that by changing work practices, work structure, and work culture in order to improve work-family integration, they can reap significant benefits in terms of productivity, employee commitment, innovation, lower turnover, and better quality. In other words, work-family integration can become a competitive advantage (Palazzi and Starcher, 2001).

Thus a *company's duty to employees* arises out of respect for the worth and dignity of individuals who devote their energies to the business and who depend on the business for their economic wellbeing. At best, the chosen strategy should promote employee's interests as concerns wage and salary levels, career opportunities, job security, and overall working conditions.

2. ***Customers:*** According to Rosabeth Moss Kanter, as quoted by Palazzi and Starcher (2001) globalisation has set in motion forces that shift power from producers who make goods to customers who buy and use them. It was a victory of market-based decision making over centrally planned economies. In market economies, *if any* single factor distinguishes the successful company or business it is putting the customer first. Successful companies build

lasting relationships with customers by focusing their whole organisation on understanding what the customers want and on providing them superior quality, reliability and service. Tom Peters refers to this as "having a passion for customers". This means building a customer perspective into all activities, including research, engineering, production, and finance, as well as selling and marketing.

A major cultural transformation is required to develop this customer focus particularly in Central and Eastern European companies and in state-owned enterprises in Western Europe now being privatized. It is thus not surprising that many companies in Eastern and Central Europe are finding it difficult to refocus their priorities on their customers. Probably the most important reason western companies are capturing markets in the former centrally planned economies is the priority which they give to developing close and responsive relationships with their customers.

But does it really pay to spend so much time and money on customers? Experience shows that companies which spend time and money on identifying what the customers want and on quality, reliability, and service are much more profitable. Armand Feigenbaum, one of the pioneers in quality management, says companies which have successful quality programmes have a 10% cost advantage over competitors: "fewer defects mean less rework and wasted management time, lower costs, and higher customer retention".

Motorola estimates that progress on quality between 1982 and 1992 saved it $ 700 million in manufacturing costs alone. Leaders in quality management are also growing faster than companies that are less conscious of this aspect of their business. Superior quality correlates closely with market share as well as with return on investment. It implies quality relationships with customers. Whereas five years ago a survey by McKinsey and Company of the reasons for success in the machinery industry showed that factors such as cross-functional teams, single sourcing, and group work differentiated the best performing companies from the weaker ones, a more recent survey concluded that what differentiates the leaders from the laggards is their relationships with their customers and their suppliers.

Today the leaders concentrate on understanding their customers in order to improve the company's value proposition and to identify new markets. They spend more time with customers (three and a half times as much for key accounts) and investigate thoroughly the reasons for lost orders. Marketing findings help to focus R & D priorities and activities.

Another reason for focusing on customers is the increasing evidence that the ethical conduct and environmental and social consciousness of companies make a difference in purchasing decisions. This evidence is supported by research of the Council on Economic Priorities (CEP), a non-profit, USA-based, public service research organisation founded in 1969 to carry out accurate and impartial analysis of the social and environmental records of corporations. The CEP information on over 700 companies and its availability empowers consumers, investors, and activists to cast their economic vote with knowledge of corporation's performance on such factors as environment, community outreach, quality of life in the workplace, information disclosure, and the advancement of women and minorities. The reputation of companies in these and other areas does influence consumers' choice of brands and producers and often leads to changing brands even if there is a price differential. Similar organisations, which perform environmental and social screening exist in Germany, United Kingdom, Switzerland, Sweden, India, and Japan. A Global Partners Working Group has been formed to disseminate and exchange company information and screening approaches (Palazzi and Starcher, 2001).

This intense focus on customers has also been referred to as "the marketing concept", which simply means that the purpose of a company is to serve customers and to satisfy their needs and desires. Under this concept, profit is a by-product, a reward for serving customers well. To achieve this, every activity of the company must be aimed at serving customers. This concept, which has been discussed in management literature for nearly fifty years, is becoming a real competitive advantage today. There is something even spiritual about this service-centered concept and the organisational implications of making it work. Clearly it implies a different degree of ethical behaviour, of honesty in respecting specifications, in describing the product and services, in advertising and in all dealings with customers.

Hence, the duty *to the customer* arises out of expectations that attend the purchase of a good or service. Should a seller inform consumers fully about the contents of its products, especially if it contains ingredients that, though officially approved for use, are suspected of having potentially harmful effects?

3. ***Suppliers:*** A Company's ethical *duty to its suppliers* arises out of the market relationship that exists between them. They are partners in the sense that the quality of suppliers' parts affect the quality of a firm's own product. They are adversaries in the sense that the supplier wants the highest price and profit it can get while the buyer wants a cheaper price, better quality, and speedier service. A company confronts several ethical issues in its supplier relationships.

In sectors characterised by intense global competition such as automobiles and consumer electronics, relationships with business partners such as suppliers and in some cases even competitors can be critically important to competitive success. As noted above, in the machinery industry, erasing the company-supplier boundary is one of the two factors, which differentiate the most successful companies. By developing long-term relationships and working closely with business partners, leaders are able to reduce complexity and costs and increase quality through joint engineering projects. Selection of suppliers is no longer exclusively through competitive bidding. A new division of labour between suppliers and customers is reinventing some industries. The nurturing of relationships with alliance and joint venture partners and with franchisees, and considering them as extensions of the company, can be equally important. This change in the strategy or policy of procurement is of great significance because many companies in Eastern and Central Europe are suppliers actual or potential for western companies. Western companies have considerably reduced the number of their suppliers and are carefully selecting those upon whom they rely. They are learning to consider their core suppliers as true partners in their business. They offer reasonable prices to ensure profitability for suppliers, they are fair in the terms and expectations, and they even involve suppliers in the new product development process. Rather than negotiating the lowest prices possible, they seek to offer fair prices, in exchange, they insist upon and receive quality and reliable delivery, and they benefit from another source of innovation. Rosabeth Moss Kanter, in her book "World Class", has offered a warning to suppliers, "As concerns suppliers and joint venture partners, being best in the neighbourhood isn't good enough anymore. Companies (as suppliers) must look good against the best in the world just to survive in the neighbourhood."

A legend in Hewlett Packard, a company noted for its good supplier relations, is about a purchasing agent who told the President that he had just negotiated a great contract with a supplier with prices reduced by 20%. The President questioned wether the supplier could make a fair profit at that price, and eventually called in the supplier to renegotiate a fairer (higher) price. Not surprisingly, the supplier became a very loyal and valuable partner to Hewlett Packard.

An excellent example of what not to do is the case of a large car manufacturer some years ago. In an attempt to cut costs, they made unreasonable demands on suppliers to reduce prices to the point that many could no longer earn a profit on their business with that company. As a result, suppliers let quality decline and put their best engineers on work for other customers. Employees of suppliers' companies quickly learned not to give that customer priority. As a result, the quality of its cars declined, as did its share of the automobile market. This was an expensive lesson for one of the world's largest corporations on how not to handle suppliers. On the positive side, TWIN is a trading organisation in the United Kingdom, which imports products from Africa. But it does not seek to maximise profits short term. TWIN pays "fair prices" and works closely with suppliers such as producers' cooperatives in Africa to develop their know-how and capacity to produce and process raw materials in a way that enhances stable employment and value added in developing countries. It stands out as a model of "fair trading" with these countries.

Another issue in developing partnerships with suppliers is human rights. Suppliers in some areas of the world violate fundamental human rights in such areas as child labour and working conditions. With increasing pressure from consumer groups, some companies are acting to insist upon respect for human rights on the part of their suppliers and are taking action to monitor performance in this area. Levi-Strauss has been a leader in this area by publishing rules of conduct expected of suppliers throughout the world and monitoring them to ensure compliance. A number of companies participated in a workshop organised by Business for Social Responsibility recently in Hong Kong on this subject of monitoring child labour practices in Asian suppliers (Palazzi and Starcher, 2001).

4. ***Communities:*** Business operates in neighbourhood, local, regional, national, and global communities. Companies can make no more important contribution to these communities, and especially to local communities, than to provide meaningful jobs, fair wages and benefits, and tax revenues. But, as 89 per cent of participants in a survey of business leaders in the United States confirmed, this is not enough. The success of business is linked to the health, stability, and prosperity of the society and of the communities in which it operates. If education is neglected, or not relevant to the needs of business, as is too often the case, companies cannot have a competitive work force. Community focused businesses like banks, retailers, and newspapers cannot prosper in declining localities. So the problems of education, health, crime, unemployment, and drugs dramatically affect business. While business has traditionally considered these to be the exclusive domain of government, today more and more business leaders are accepting part of the responsibility to improve the communities in which they do business. Companies relate to communities in various ways. For illustration:

   *(a)* ***Charity:*** Charitable contributions are only the tip of the iceberg, but are nevertheless important. These can be from the company itself or though facilitation or matching of employee contributions. Employee volunteerism for community-building projects enhances employee loyalty and can contribute to the personal development of some employees. Leadership potential

and other valuable skills are sometimes discovered outside the company on such projects. In the United States, corporate support of the arts and private education is critically important. In Europe, corporations have contributed importantly to such causes as the preservation of the architectural heritage.

(b) ***Social investment:*** At another level, companies support initiatives in the areas of education and social problems such as unemployment, exclusion, and homelessness, often in partnership with government authorities and non-governmental organisations. Corporate involvement in the Brussels-based European Business Network for Social Cohesion and in projects to alleviate social exclusion is exemplary, as is the support of hundreds of the largest companies in the United Kingdom for the notable achievements of such associations as Business in the Community, the Prince of Wales Business Leaders Forum, and Common Purpose.

(c) ***Partnerships:*** At a third level, corporations contribute to communities through direct support to activities, which enhance their commercial success, including cause-related marketing. These activities are often in partnership with other social partners. "Being a good citizen in our communities is one of our core corporate values" says Harvey Golub, Chairman of American Express Company. He notes two trends in community involvement. The first, which American Express pioneered, is cause-related marketing. One example is a recent bold commitment of $ 5 million to the World Monuments Fund to help restore and preserve some of the world's endangered cultural sites. The link with the core travel and financial service activities of the company is obvious. The second trend is linking charitable contributions to employee involvement. American Express created the Volunteer Action Fund in 1994 to award grants to eligible organisations (worldwide) at which its employees regularly volunteer their time.

*(d)* ***Business basics:*** Finally, and most importantly, business contributes to communities and to society through its fundamental mission of providing products and services which society needs and wants in an efficient and ethical manner and in a way that respects and balances the interests of all stakeholders. Examples of corporate community involvement in these four areas abound. One of the leaders is Grand Metropolitan, one of the world's leading consumer goods companies, specializing in branded food and drink businesses (Pillsbury, Green Giant, Haagen-Dazs, Burger King, Smirnoff, Cinzano, Heublein). GrandMet has just published a remarkable Report on Corporate Citizenship 1997 describing its commitment and philosophy in this area. This report describes seven specific case studies of its community involvement in the United Kingdom, the United States, India, and South Africa. It also describes an innovative reporting and measurement process, including benchmarking and feedback, for assessing achievements of their community relations objectives.

There is a considerable difference in approaches between cultures and companies. In France, a number of leading groups such as Lafltrge, Saint Gobain, and Schneider have developed innovative approaches to job creation to avoid layoffs during necessary restructuring. To alleviate high unemployment, some of these same groups have entered into partnerships with national, regional, and local government authorities in apprenticeship and education programmes to facilitate insertion of youth into the workforce (Palazzi and Starcher, 2001).

Thus, we see that a Company's *duty to the community at large* stems from its status as the citizen of the community and as an institution of society. The community and public interest should be accorded the same recognition and attention as the other four constituencies. Whether a company is a good community citizen is ultimately demonstrated by the way it supports community activities, encourages employees to participate in community activities, handles the health and safety aspects of its operations, accepts responsibility for overcoming environmental pollution, relates to regulatory bodies and employee unions, and exhibits high ethical standards (Thompson and Strickland, 1995)

## Ethics and Competitiveness—Putting First Things First

It is quite often alleged that corporations do not stick to ethical practices as it reduces the options available before them and thus pulls down the competitiveness. However, the managers striving to succeed in an increasingly interdependent world with the potential for improved living standards for all should think not just as managers focussing on a narrow preserve labeled business ethics but as citizens of a larger society.

Ethics and competitiveness are inseparable. We compete as a society and no society anywhere will compete very long or successfully with people stabbing each other in the back; with people trying to steal from each other; with everything requiring notarized confirmation because you can't trust the other fellow; with every little squabble ending in litigation; and with government writing reams of regulatory legislation, tying business hand and foot to keep it honest. This is a recipe not only for headaches in running a company; it is a recipe for a nation to become wasteful, inefficient, and noncompetitive. There is no escaping this fact: the greater the measure of mutual trust and confidence in the ethics of a society, the greater its economic strength.

All human beings are endowed with a moral sense—the average farmer behind a plow can decide a moral question as well as a university professor. That common moral sense, however, does not come out of nowhere or perpetuate itself automatically. Every generation must keep it alive and flourishing. All of us can think of means to this end. John F Akers (1989) proposes two suggestions:

1. *Ethical Buttresses*: First, we should fortify the practical ethical buttresses that help all of us—from childhood on- know, understand and do exactly what is required of us. The simplest and most powerful buttress is the role model: parents and others who by precept and example set us straight on good and evil, right and wrong. However, for our purposes, it is the institutionalized buttresses and the professional standards and business codes of conducts,

which spell out strict policies on such things as insider trading, gifts and entertainment, kickbacks and conflict of interest that promise to help. It is naïve to believe these buttresses will solve all our problems. But it is equally naive to expect ethical behaviour to occur in the absence of clear requirements and consequences.

2. *First Things First*: We should keep our sense of order straight. Let's put first things first. We have all heard shortsighted business people attribute a quotation to Vince Lombardi: "Winning is not the most important thing; it's the only thing." That's good quotation for firing up a team, but as a business philosophy it is sheer nonsense. There is another much better Lombardi quotations. He once said he expected his players to have three kinds of loyalty: to God, to their families, and to the Green Pay Packers, "in that order". He knew that some things count more than others. Businessmen and women can be unabashedly proud of their companies. But the good of an entire society transcends that of any single corporation (p. 70).

## Tapping the Commitment of the Employees

A dramatic shift in priorities is distinctly visible among companies that are becoming aware of the dichotomy between personal values and professional life. With so many individuals seeking change, and some opting out of the 'rat race', companies and organisations are struggling with two critical and interrelated management issues: How to retain the best people and improve productivity. Neal (1999) writes, "...we are actually in the midst of an important paradigm shift as the last vestiges of defunct industrial era practices prepare to fall. We are experiencing the beginning of a transformation in the workplace. This is not the latest fad but a genuine recognition that the workplace has an important role to play in our need for wholeness and integration" (p. 28).

This paves the way for a conscious-business movement in which the organisations for its survival provides a learning community to the employees who work in and develops business-social partnership to serve the society. The people of an organisation constitute its core resource for continuing competitiveness. This resource comprises people's individual and collective learning and knowledge, skills and expertise, creativity and innovation, competencies and capabilities i.e. people's continuous capacity for providing customer-valued outcomes. In terms of their continual enhancement of such a capacity. The people of an enterprise constitute an appreciating resource i.e. its human capital. The primary challenge in such a changed politico-economic environment becomes to encourage the new, better-educated work force to be: Committed, Self-managing and Life-long learners. This is becomes possible when the organisation sustains itself as a community.

## Sustaining Organisations as Communities

The word 'community' has old roots, going back to the Indo-European base *mei* meaning 'change' or 'exchange". Apparently this joined with another root, *kom* meaning 'with', to produce an Indo-European word *kommein:* shared by all. The idea of 'change or exchange shared by all' seems to be very close to the sense of community in organisation to day. Community building is a core strategy for sharing among all its members the burden and the benefits of change and exchange (Senge, 1994).

The 21$^{st}$ century communities have been the most powerful mechanisms for creating human co-operation and reliable interdependence. In order to involve the people and tap their potential organisations need to provide a nurturing environment, which is necessary for maintaining the health, vitality, and productivity of the people who will interact directly with the organisation throughout its life. The reconception of organisation as communities does not mean throwing out of the entreprenurial spirit of the business world. Instead, it provides the chance to merge the best of the community traditions with the best of the free-enterprise system. In the coming years a combined organisation-community form can produce better performance than any of the traditional forms of organisation. But it needs to be designed not only to support the personal experience of community, but also to assure the long-term sustainability of community.

The action techniques for this work emerged from the community development movement and from voluntary organisation. Paulo Freire's work in Brazilian education, the tradition of Scandinavian study circles, and the community activism of Saul Alnisky's Industrial Areas Foundation are key influences. Mahatma Gandhi, Martin Luther King Jr., and Cesar Chavez were all gifted leaders in designing creative approaches for engaging large numbers of people to work together toward a shared vision of a better future.

The concept of community organisation is rooted solidly in our democratic traditions, in which people live and support each other to serve the common good, as well as their individual interests. The question arises, how can we bring such practices into our business organisations which can help to tap the same community tradition of service, informed participation and contribute to the common good.

To realize this organisations need to have a caring culture where the members freely interact and have a free frank dialogues, both vertically as well as horizontally. There are six core processes highlighted by Senge (1992) and adopted in the present study for creating and sustaining organisations as communities.

*(a) Capability:* Vital Communities are capable because they have the skills, knowledge and personal qualities to renew themselves and reinvent their future.

*(b) Commitment:* Builds when people are an active part of the experiences or creating something they value together. To build community in an organisation under the stress of unrelenting change, mutual commitment becomes important: what commitment the organisation is asking of its employees and what commitments will the organisation make and keep in return?

*(c) Contribution:* It is important to develop ways for people to see clearly how their daily work makes a real contribution to the organisation's success. Business Process Improvement incorporates this concept. However, unless it is seen as one key to building community, people feel like they have been re-engineered, rather than the work process.

(d) ***Continuity:*** Communities cannot survive without some measure of "continuity". If we want to gain the benefits of healthy communities in the workplace, we need to become more creative about how to build some sources of continuity.

(e) ***Collaboration:*** Developing reliable inter-dependence is the essence of effective collaboration in a community. In new interactive forums of strategic planning, people gather regularly to share information about progress and clarify direction, in an ongoing organisation-wide collaborative learning process.

(f) ***Conscience:*** All healthy communities incorporate processes, which could be described as "conscience" mechanisms. The organisation finds ways to embody or invoke guiding principles, ethics, and values such as service, trust and mutual respect. These, in turn, translate into daily actions and concrete decisions. But most organisational conscience mechanisms are tacit. Even when there is a value or mission statement, the question, "To what are we going to be responsible?" is rarely raised explicitly. Community building brings that question to the surface. Exploring the question of conscience is a first step toward repositioning the organisation within its larger community.

The workplace has become an increasingly complex and competitive environment. The demands of a global economy and the proliferation of technology have forced many organisations to restructure and adopt more flexible strategies that focus on core processes and competencies (Hamel and Prahalad, 1989; Prahalad and Hamel, 1990), market orientation and customer responsiveness (Day, 1994; Slater and Narver, 1995), and quality initiativeness (Gehani, 1993). Because products and services can be easily replicated and reproduced, organisations are being increasingly challenged to leverage learning through knowledge creation, dissemination and continuous innovation (Nonaka, 1991). Stata (1989) has argued that "the rate at which individuals and organisations learn may become the only source of sustainable competitive advantage" (p. 64).

Not only is the institutionalized competency of active learning a strategic imperative but it is also a powerful fringe benefit for the employees who work there. Organisations need to identify the creative individuals and then protect and nurture their talents in order to enable them to perform up to their potential (Smith, et al., 2000). This helps in attracting and retaining good employees. One of the things that attract employees to an organisation is their perception that the organisation is headed for success and is willing to invest in its employees along the way. Helping the employees gain new skills or deepen their current capabilities is a powerful way in which organisations can show their future commitment and investment in the people. Helping the employees to learn is viewed as a powerful fringe benefit.

Thus creating the learning capability within the organisation and instilling the capability at every level in the organisation provides a double benefit: its both a strategic advantage as well as a powerful fringe benefit (Kahle, 2000).

## The Research Issues

Against this background the author advocates a reflective perspective in order to mirror the organisational existentialism for sustainable competitive advantage. The organisations should continuously do a SWOT analysis for itself. If the organisations continuously think over its existence in terms of—Who are we? What are we responsible for? What are we doing? etc. etc. then this will help them in maintaining their sustainability. To realise this, the organisation requires bringing people together and enabling them to mobilize their collective efforts.

This suggests a systemic thinking. Organisations can no longer be considered as separate entity rather as social entities. Therefore, how they connect themselves to the larger community becomes very important. The social responsibilities philosophy of the organisations need to be more than the philanthropy. Not only this, the organisation practising the social responsibility philosophy should have a well structured credos along with the mission statement for its organisation, so that the workplace constitution protects the rights of organisational citizens and multiple stakeholder satisfaction is valued and practiced by that organisation. Regardless of the economic achievements businesses must abide by established laws and regulations in order to be good citizens. The establishment of strict ethical standards in the workplace may also be an excellent way to prevent legal violations by creating a focus on integrity on decision making. The credo of the organisation is likely to help in taking practical decisions. This is likely to enhance the employees' personal integrity and accountability towards the organisation. Employees in every organisation want to give, especially, if it appears to them meaningful and worthwhile. Therefore, in order to tap the commitment and the potential of the employees for the organisational improvement the managers need to adopt certain clear-cut practices as to what sort of commitment the company/organisation wants from its employees and what commitment will the organisation/company make in return.

The present book addresses some of these issues in Indian organisations.

# Chapter—2

# METHODOLOGY

## Objective of the Study

Against this framework the present study intends to examine the extent to which organisations use conscience mechanisms for providing a healthy workplace and meeting their social responsibilities. It is assumed that to exemplify this pursuit organisations need to have fair organisational practices, which in turn will provide personal integrity to the employees in terms of scope for learning and development and a real zeal to serve the public interest by making investment for social development.

## Measures

A structured schedule was used for the purpose. The variables taken into account seem to fall into two broad categories:

### (1) Individual Level Factors

*(a) Attitude towards Business Ethics Questionnaire:* Whether the manager acts ethically or unethically is the result of a complex interaction between individual characteristics, structural variables and organisation's culture. The scale developed by Arie Reichel and Yoram Neumann (1988) was adopted in the present study. The sale had 18 items. The responses were obtained on a 5-point scale where Strongly Agree means 5, Agree means 4, Neither Agree Nor Disagree means 3, Disagree means 2 and Strongly Disagree means 1. The scores ranged

from 1-5 on each item. The reliability coefficient of the scale was reported to be. 77.

(b) ***Value checklist:*** The value checklist used by Senge et al (1994) was adopted to examine the most significant value of the respondents. A list of 84 values (work and personal) was given to respondents with an instruction to select the most important one by the eliminating process.

(c) ***Personal Integrity Scale:*** The perception of personal integrity was examined in terms of scope for learning within the organisation and the extent to which employees' seemed to share the long-term perspective of the organisation. A six-item scale was used for the purpose. The respondents were asked to judge the chances of its occurrences in their respective organisation on a 5-point percentage scale by encircling any one. The minimum score on each item was 0% and maximum 100%. The reliability of the scale was measured and the alpha coefficients were found to be. 65.

## (2) Organisation Level Factors

(a) ***Organisational Culture and Socio-Cultural Context:*** The scale developed by Hofstede and used by Dorfman (1988) was adopted in the present study with necessary modifications. The scale that was used in the present study had 25 items. The respondents were asked to judge each statement on a 5-point scale of agreement-disagreement. The anchor points were *Strongly Agree* (5), *Agree* (4), *Neither Agree nor Disagree* (3), *Disagree* (2) and *Strongly Disagree* (1). The minimum score on each item was 1 and maximum 5. The obtained reliability value of the scale was. 73.

(b) ***Sustaining Organisations as Communities:*** A six-item scale was used to operationalize the items pertaining to capability, commitment, contribution, continuity, collaboration, and conscience (as mentioned in Chapter—1). The respondents were asked to judge each statement on a 5 point scale ranging from Great Extent (5) to Not at all (1) The scale had an alpha value of. 79.

*(c)* ***Organisational Improvement Questionnaire:*** Some open ended items were used to examine the nature of commitment the company/organisation wants from its employees and will make in return which was assumed to be important for organisational improvement. The respondents were asked to write down their views on:

*(i)* What sort of commitment is the organisation asking of its employees?

*(ii)* What commitments will the organisation make and keep in return?

The respondents were further asked,

*(iii)* Please indicate the relative importance of personal self-interest and collective enterprise.

*(iv)* Focus of the organisation is to promote

- Personal self-interest of the employees, how?
- Collective enterprise, how?

*(d)* ***Employees' Contribution Measure:*** In every organisation people want to give, especially, if it is to something they think is needed and worthwhile. That is why it is important to develop ways for people to see clearly how their daily work makes a real contribution to organisation success. A three-item scale was used to examine the chances of the three mechanisms favoured in the organisation on a 5-point scale (0%-100%). The three mechanisms were:

**(a) Free Agency;**

**(b) Employment Stability;**

**(c) Community Boundaries**

The alpha coefficients of the scale were reported to be.59.

*(e)* ***Innovativeness, Learning Community and Sustainability:*** If we want to gain the benefits of healthy communities in the workplace, we need to become more creative about how to build some sources of continuity. A four-item scale was used to examine

how the continuity is maintained. The responses were obtained on a 5-point scale. The scores ranged from 1-5 on each item. The reliability score of the scale was found to be.56.

(f) ***Perception of Ethical Work Climate:*** Three items were used to tap the responses with regard to perception of ethical work climate within the organisation. One was open-ended item where the respondents were asked to jot down their views on.

What mechanism do you have to protect membership entitlements? Please jot down your views.

The other two were framed into a 5-point scale. The respondents were to rate,

(1) To what extent workplace constitution protects the rights of organisational citizens?

| Not at All | Little Extent | Can not Say | Some Extent | Great Extent |
|---|---|---|---|---|

(2) The employees of this organisation are more concerned for their rights than their responsibilities.

| Quite True | True | Can not Say | Some Extent | Great Extent |
|---|---|---|---|---|

(g) ***Organisational Existentialism Scale:*** The scale consisted of items related to company's mission statement, guiding principles, credos, responsible decision making and social responsibility of the organisations. The author developed this scale. It is a combination of open-ended items and Likert type scale.

(h) ***Business Strategy:*** The author was interested in examining how do the companies select their business strategies. Therefore, the respondents were asked to respond to three open-ended questions:

*(a)* What are the criteria for weeding out candidate strategies?

*(b)* How can a manager judge which strategic option is best for the company?

(*c*) What are the standards for determining whether a strategy is successful or not?

(*i*) ***Organisational Citizenship Behaviour:*** The respondents were asked,

(*a*) To what extent multiple stakeholder satisfaction and involvement is valued and practised in your organisation?

The ratings were obtained on a 5-point scale. The responses ranged from *Great Extent* (5) to *Some Extent* (4) through *Cannot Say* (3) *Little Extent* (2) to *Not at All* (1).

Attempts were further made to examine organisation's policy with respect to its each stakeholder in terms of *objective* and *relationship*. Therefore, a open-ended item was put to tap the views of the respondents. *They were given the instruction:*

Please respond to the following in terms of your organisation's policy to satisfy their expectations:

**(1) Customers**

*Your objective*

*Your relationship*

**(2) Shareholders**

*Your objective*

*Your relationship*

**(3) Employees**

*Your objective*

*Your relationship*

**(4) Suppliers**

*Your objective*

*Your relationship*

**(5) Communities**

*Your objective*

*Your relationship*

### (3) Background Information

Some items related to respondent's age, educational qualification, level in the organisation, size of the organisation, etc. were sought to have the background of the respondents.

## The Sample

A total number of 135 respondents participated in the study. Out of these 36% of the respondents were working in small sized organisations and 64% in the large sized ones. The respondents were from varied age groups. 21.4 per cent reported to be between 25-30 years, 25.2 per cent between 31-39 years, 31.9 per cent between 40-49 years, 18.5 per cent between 50-59 years and 3.0 per cent above 60 years. The educational qualification of the majority of the respondents (57.8%) seemed to be post-graduation. 28.9 per cent of the respondents reported to be graduates. A very marginal number said to be diploma holders (5.9%), Ph.D. (5.2%) and having professional degrees (2.2%). About 49.6% of the respondents reported Business as their main discipline of education whereas 34.1% reported it to be Applied Science. A Marginal percentage of respondents (16.3%) were found to have Social Science as their educational discipline. The sample constituted of senior (39.2%), middle (48.9%) and junior (11.9%) level managers. 58.5% of the respondents reported to spent their early lives (first twenty-five years) in Eastern India, 15.6% spent it in Northern India, 18.5% reported it to be Western India, 3% reported to spent their early lives in Southern India and 4.4% in a mixed setting. Out of these respondents 55.5% spend their childhood in joint family, 40% in nuclear family, 3% in hostels and 1.5% in hostels as well as in nuclear family.

## The Setting

The study was conducted in the Eastern and Western-Southern parts of India. Five organisations provided the settings for the present research:

1. Gujrat Ambuja Group of Companies, Calcutta;
2. Usha Martin, Calcutta;
3. Excel Industries Limited, Mumbai;

4. Godrej and Boyce Manufacturing Company Limited, Mumbai;

5. Bank of Baroda, Calcutta.

The organisations varied in the nature of work that they performed, however, all seemed to do some amount of social responsibilities towards the community. Most of these organisations believed in simplicity and fair practices. Ethical practices seemed to be emphasized and practised.

The rationale behind selecting such organisations was that those practising ethical norms is likely to be involved in social development activities and the organisation involved in social development activities may practice ethical norms and fair organisational practices.

## The Procedure

The Vice-Presidents of the companies were sent a formal request letter for seeking their permission to conduct the study in their respective companies. The data were collected from December 1999—August 2000. The investigator invested sufficient time in interviewing and observing the people. Apart from using the schedule informal interviews were conducted in order to have a better understanding of the related issues.

# Chapter—3
# RESULTS

The present study is aimed at examining the conscience mechanisms that organisations adopt in order to retain their workforce and enhance productivity. This can be realized by (a) developing one's organisation as a community where people feel involved and committed and (b) interconnecting itself with the larger community. The focus of the study was not to examine the organisational differences but to know the overall trend; therefore, the analyses were done on the total sample.

## Individual Level Factors

*(1)* ***Attitude towards Business Ethics:*** The scale had 18 items, which were factor analyzed. The factors above. 40 were taken into account. The factor along with its loading were presented in Appendix—I. The descriptive statistics were computed on the factor scores and entered in Table—1.

**Table—1**
**Mean and SD Scores of the Factors Related to Attitude towards Business Ethics**

| | *Factors* | *Mean Scores* | *SD Scores* |
|---|---|---|---|
| 1. | Maximizing benefits | 18.80 | 5.70 |
| 2. | Emphasis on competitiveness and profitability | 16.25 | 2.43 |
| 3. | Fair practices | 8.73 | 2.28 |
| 4. | Rational decision | 3.56 | 1.00 |
| 5. | Business world has its own rules | 3.76 | 0.93 |

Note. N = 135.

The mean scores reported in Table—1 suggested that the respondents' attitude towards business ethics seemed to be that maximizing benefits. The respondents emphasized on competitiveness and profitability. The former was given a priority over the latter. Ethics as such was found not to be given much importance as the respondents believed that the business in making money and therefore there is no place for ethics and moral values as business need economic attitudes. However the respondents' stressed the importance of legal practices.

Once can have a better understanding of the findings from Figure—1.

**Figure—1**
**Attitude Towards Business**

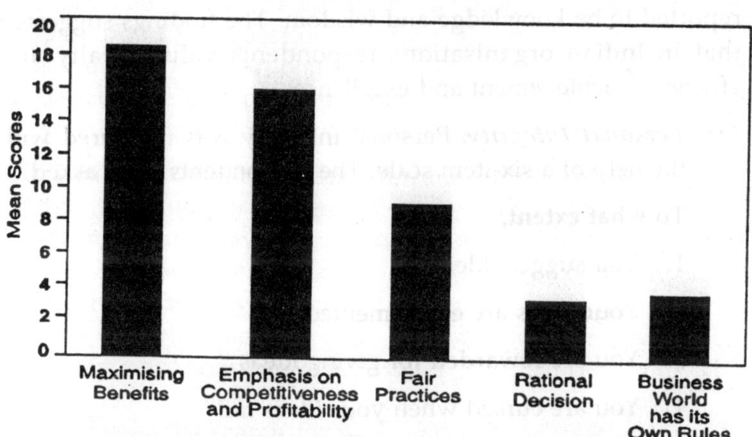


(2) ***Personal Values:*** The respondents were asked to select one value, which they most strongly felt, by the eliminating process. The percentages of responses on the preferred personal values are graphically presented in Figure—2.

Figure—2 highlighted two dominant values preferred by the respondents; Honesty and truth and achievement, excellence and efficiency. Self-respect, integrity, knowledge and wisdom were found to have very low percentages. The most preferred value seemed to be honesty and truth and least preferred one was

Figure—2
Preferred Personal Values

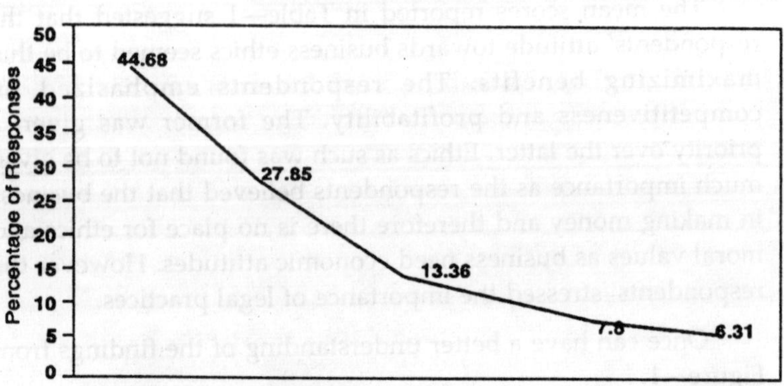


reported to be knowledge and wisdom. The findings suggested that in Indian organisations respondents value loyalty and efficiency, achievement and excellence.

(3) *Personal Integrity*: Personal integrity was measured with the help of a six-item scale. The respondents were asked,

To what extent,

1. You suggest ideas
2. Your ideas are experimented
3. You are rewarded for giving ideas
4. You are cursed when your ideas fail
5. You can develop multi-skills
6. Initiativeness is valued

The results disclosed that 46.7 per cent of the respondents were found to suggest ideas (75% of the time) against 14.1 per cent who said the chances to be 25% and 17% who reported it to be 100%. 22.2 per cent of the respondents seemed to be of the view that chances for suggesting ideas are 50%. On the issue of ideas being experimented, a major chunk of respondents (37 per cent) reported it to be 50%. Interestingly, negligible percentage said it to be either 0% (1.5 per cent) or 100% (6.7 per cent). 25.9 per cent of the respondents reported the chances to be 25% against 28.9 per cent who said it to be 75%. The interesting finding came up while they responded to the item related to being rewarded for giving ideas. 29.6 per cent told the chances to be 0% against 7.4% who reported the chances to be 100%. Further, 27.4 per cent said it to be 25%, 21.5 per cent reported it to be 50% and 14.1 per cent to be 75%. The results suggested that the employees were neither rewarded nor cursed for suggesting ideas. 42.2 per cent of the respondents said that they were not cursed when their ideas fail, however, 25.2 per cent were of view that 25% of the chances they were cursed for it. Interestingly, 5.2 per cent of the respondents expressed that they were always cursed against 9.6 and 17.8 percentages that reported it to be 75% and 50% respectively. The extent to which the organisation provides scope for developing multiple skills is very important for the perception of personal integrity. The findings were quite affirmative. 33.3 per cent of the respondents were of the view that they were able to develop multiple skills 50% of the chances and 34.1 percentage reported the chances to be 75%. To add, 19.3 per cent of the respondents told that the organisation provided 100% chances to develop multi skills against 13.3 per cent that found it to be 25%. The another important dimension of this perceived personal integrity is the extent to which the employees shared long-term perspectives by taking initiatives. The results highlighted that 24.4 per cent of the respondents were of opinion that the initiativeness is always valued (100%). A good number of respondents (34.1 per cent) reported it to be 75%. On the contrary 1.5 per cent expressed it to be 0%, 17.8 per cent to be 25% and 22.2 per cent to be 50% chances when initiativeness is valued in the organisation.

The obtained mean scores on these six dimensions are graphically portrayed in Figure—3.

Figure—3
Personal Integrity as an Indicator of Employees' Contribution to Organisational Success

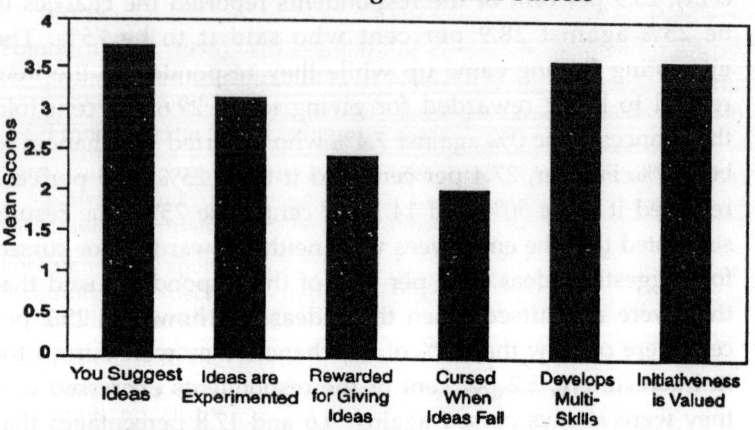


## Organisation Level Factors

*(1) Organisational Culture and Socio-Cultural Context:* The analyses were made in two different ways. One by using Hofstede's four dimensions and the other by examining the emerging factors.

(a) *Using Hofstede's culture dimensions:* The obtained mean scores are entered into Table—2.

Table—2
Mean and SD Scores of the Organisational Culture and Socio-Cultural Context on Hofstede's Dimensions

| | *Dimensions* | *Mean Scores* | *SD Scores* |
|---|---|---|---|
| 1. | Uncertainty—Avoidance | 22.08 | 1.89 |
| 2. | Individual—Collectivism | 19.92 | 2.58 |
| 3. | Power Distance | 14.61 | 3.95 |
| 4. | Masculinity-Femininity | 23.63 | 5.61 |

Note. N = 135.

Table—2 indicated that Indian organisations seemed to have a masculine culture which showed employees attached importance to earnings, recognition and advancement with men.

Further, the reported mean score for uncertainty-avoidance indicated the presence of such culture which tend to have more emotional resistance to change, weaker achievement motivation, a preference for specialist career over managerial and a fear of failure. The findings (as reported in Table—2) disclosed low Individualism score that in the case of collectivist societies indicates the presence of an emotional dependence on the company, managers aspire to conformity and orderliness, group decisions are considered better than the individual ones, and managers value security in their work. Interestingly, Power Distance was found to be low which suggested that managers tend to consult their subordinates when making decisions, perceived work ethic is stronger, close supervisions evaluated negatively by subordinates, and employees are co-operative.

*(b)* ***Factor analyses:*** Nine factors emerged out of the factor analyses. The factors along with its loading were presented in Appendix—II. The items having the factor loading above than .40 were taken into account. To name the factors.

*(1)* ***Authoritative,*** which constituted of items, i.e., *Managers should not delegate difficult and important tasks to their subordinates. It is more important for men to have a professional career than it is for women. Women do not value recognition and promotion in their work as much as men do.*

*(2)* ***Power Orientation*** Comprised items, i.e., *Rules and regulations are important because they inform the worker what the organisation expects of them. It is important for manager to encourage loyalty and a sense of duty to the group etc.*

*(3)* ***Normative Behaviour*** had the items, i.e., *It is important to have job requirements and instructions spelled out so people always know what they are expected to do. Individual rewards are not as important as group welfare. There are some jobs which a man can always do better than a women.*

*(4)* ***Power Distance*** Constituted of items, i.e., *Managers should take most decisions without consulting subordinates. It is often necessary for a superior to emphasize his or her authority and power when dealing with subordinates.*

(5) ***Stereotyped Perception*** was formed with the items, i.e., *Men usually solve problems with logical analysis, and women solve problems with intuition. Solving organisational problems usually requires the active forcible approach, which is typical of men etc.*

(6) ***Job Clarity*** was explained with items, i.e., *Standard operating procedures are helpful to workers on the job. Instructions for operations are important for workers on the job etc.*

(7) ***Acceptance in Group*** had a single item-*Being accepted by the group is more important than working on your own.*

(8) ***Social Relationship*** comprised two items *A Manager should avoid socializing with his or her subordinates off the job and Women are more concerned with social aspects of their job than they are with getting ahead.*

(9) ***Sex Based Managerial Styles*** had two items—*Managers expect workers to closely follow instructions and procedures and women value working in a friendly atmosphere than men do.*

The factor mean scores are quoted in Table—3.

**Table—3**

**Mean and SD Scores of the Factors related to Perception of Organisational Culture and Socio-Cultural Context**

| | *Factors* | *Mean Scores* | *SD Scores* |
|---|---|---|---|
| 1. | Authoritative | 6.50 | 2.36 |
| 2. | Power Orientation | 11.81 | 1.80 |
| 3. | Normative Behaviour | 17.17 | 3.09 |
| 4. | Power Distance | 9.90 | 3.03 |
| 5. | Stereotyped Perception | 11.00 | 1.23 |
| 6. | Job Clarity | 8.71 | 1.35 |
| 7. | Acceptance in Group | 4.44 | .74 |
| 8. | Social Relationships | 4.99 | 1.56 |
| 9. | Sex-Based Managerial Styles | 7.55 | 1.37 |

Note. N = 135

Table—3 showed a preference for normative behaviour and power orientation in the organisations. The perceived organisational culture seemed to have the spill over of stereotyped socio-cultural perceptions. This clearly indicates the influence of national culture on organisational behaviour.

***(2) Sustaining Organisations as Communities:*** The scale measured the six core processes (as discussed earlier), Capability, Contribution, Commitment, Continuity, Collaborations and Conscience. Table—4 contained the mean and SD scores.

**Table—4**
**Mean and SD Scores of the Variables Related to the Variables Regarding Sustaining Organisations as Communities**

| | *Variables* | *Mean Scores* | *SD Scores* |
|---|---|---|---|
| 1. | Capability | 3.89 | 0.96 |
| 2. | Contribution | 3.46 | 1.00 |
| 3. | Commitment | 4.04 | 1.07 |
| 4. | Continuity | 4.19 | 0.97 |
| 5. | Collaboration | 3.84 | 0.99 |
| 6. | Conscience Mechanism | 3.18 | 1.22 |

Note. N = 135.

Table—4 indicated that the respondents perceived the organisational climate to be supportive in maintaining some amount of continuity. Commitment and continuity were found to be operative to some extent. Interestingly, the organisations seemed low in terms of tapping the capability of the employees. As a result, the employees may not feel that the organisation inspires their best thinking. Further, the respondents reported their organisations to be low on conscience mechanisms.

(3) ***Organisational Improvement Measures:*** To sustain the Competitive advantage the organisations need to do a SWOT analysis for themselves.

***(a) Commitment: The Organisation Wants:*** An open-ended item was used to ascertain the views of the respondents on the commitments the organisation was asking for from its employees. The obtained responses were content analysed and the findings are portrayed in Figure—4.

Firuge—4
Commitment: The Organisation is Asking For

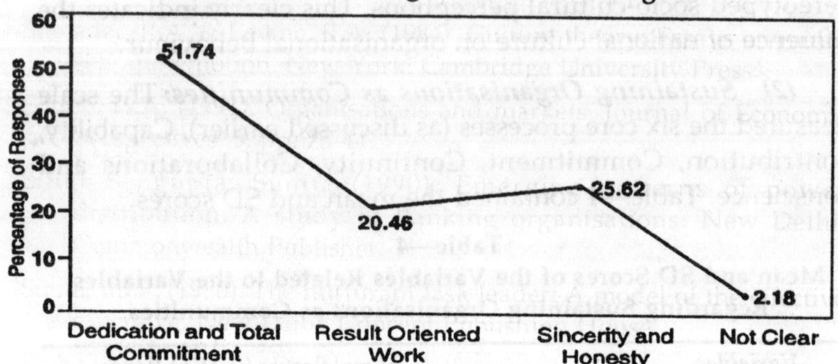


Figure—4 clearly indicated that the organisation wants dedication and total commitment of the employees towards organisational goals by emphasizing honesty and sincerity through best efforts, innovativeness and result oriented work.

*(b) Commitments: The Organisation will Keep in Return.* What commitments will the organisation make and keep in return? The responses were obtained for it, which were content analyzed and graphically represented in Figure—5.

Figure—5
Commitments: The Organisation will Make and Keep in Return

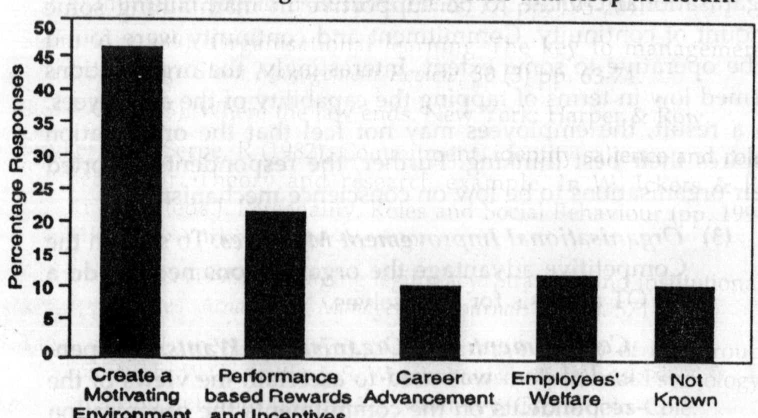

Figure—5 highlighted that the organisation's commitment towards the employees is in terms of creating a motivating environment by providing challenging and interesting opportunities. A good number of respondents (10.34%) said that organisations make no commitment. 22.5 per cent of the respondents were of opinion that organisations keep their commitments through performance-based rewards and incentives. 11.02 percentage of respondents considered employees' welfare activities to be the commitment kept by the organisation in return. Interestingly, only 10.11 per cent of respondents reported career advancement of the employees to be the commitment kept by the organisations in return.

(c) ***Personal Interest vis-a-vis Collective Enterprise:*** The obtained responses were content analyzed and the finding indicated that the respondents considered personal interest to be a motivator, however, while responding to personal interest and collective enterprise they expressed the views that personal interest and collective interest go hand in hand without disturbing each other. The finding hinted the feeling of the respondents that collective enterprise should be given priority over personal interest.

On the issue, how does organisations promote personal/collective interest it was reported that the focus of the organisations is to encourage individual efforts by providing performance-based rewards. On the other hand the nature of work demands teamwork. The question arises, how can we merge the personal interest with the broader collective interest of the organisations.

***(4) Employees' Contribution Measure***

(a) ***Free Agency:*** The item was related with the chances that employees could seek and accept the position anywhere in the global enterprise without fear of local reprisal. The obtained results suggested the chances to be between 25%—50% (as reported by 53.3 per cent of the respondents). Some (25.2 per cent of respondents) reported the chances to be 100% but they then informally said that it hardly happens. 10.4 per cent of the respondents told the chances to be 0% and 11.1 per cent to be 75%.

(b) ***Employment Stability:*** 40% of the respondents perceived the employment stability to be 75 per cent. A small group of respondents (0.7 per cent) told the employment stability to be 0% against 30.4 per cent the respondents who said it to be 100 per cent.

(c) ***Community Boundaries:*** were examined by the chances of the processes favoured in the organisation by which membership is extended to newcomers or withdrawn and the processes by which community-wide standards for members were developed and maintained. The findings indicated the prevalence of such a process to be 50 per cent (as reported by 44.4% of the respondents) 28.1% of them (respondents) thought it to be 75 per cent.

***(5) Innovativeness, Learning Community and Sustainability***

The descriptive analyses computed are entered in Table—5.

**Table—5**
**Mean and SD of the Measures Related to Innovativeness, Learning Community and Sustainability**

| | *Measures* | *Mean Scores* | *SD Scores* |
|---|---|---|---|
| 1. | Stories and folklore used to highlight success efforts | 3.56 | 1.18 |
| 2. | Help the new members to understand the rights, responsi-bilities and practices of the learning community | 3.46 | 1.03 |
| 3. | Chances of Rotating Leadership at very senior levels | 2.54 | 0.98 |
| 4. | Develop a sense of Collective Identity | 3.18 | 0.86 |

Note. N = 135.

Table—5 indicated that the organisations seemed to help the new members to understand the rights, responsibilities and practices of the learning community to some extent. Sometimes the successes were highlighted in terms of stories and folklore. The respondents favoured the chances (somewhat between 50-75 per cent) that the challenge for global corporations will be to develop a sense of collective identity. The chances of rotating leadership at the top seemed to be very low.

One can have a better understanding on each measure from Figures 6,7,8 & 9.

**Figure—6**
**Measures of Continuity: Stories and Folklore**

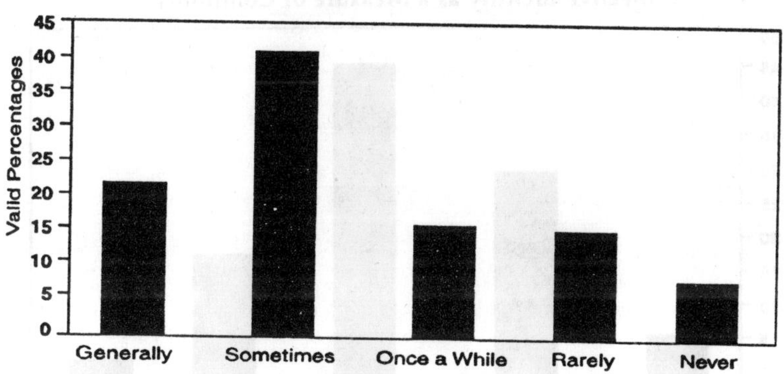


**Figure—7**
**Measures of Continuity: A Learning Community**

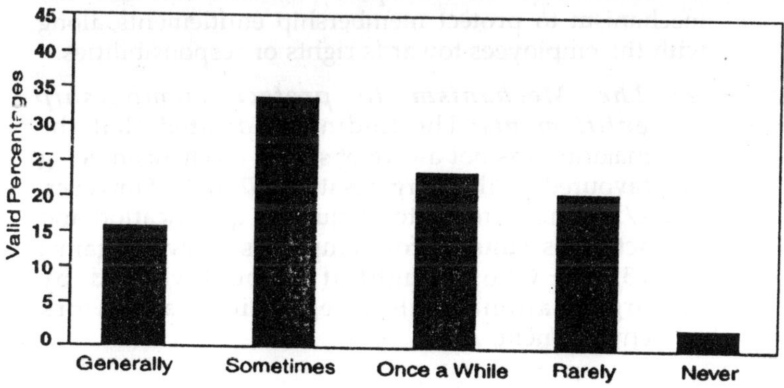

Figure—8
Rotating Leadership as a Measure of Continuity

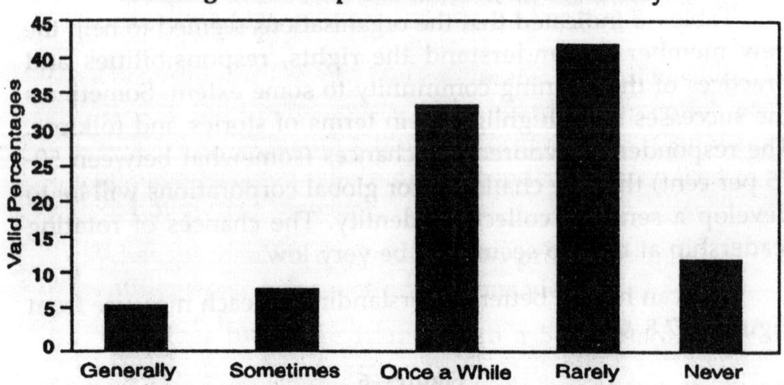


Figure—9
Collective Identity as a Measure of Continuity

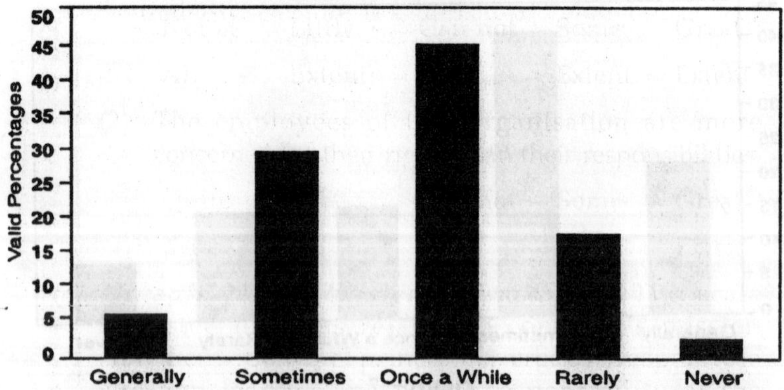


***(6) Perception of Ethical work Climate:*** Efforts were made to understand the workplace constitution and the mechanism to protect membership entitlements along with the employees towards rights or responsibilities.

***(a) The Mechanism to protect membership entitlements:*** The findings indicated that the majority was not aware of such a mechanism being favoured by their organisation (52.02%). However, 27.58% reported it to be quality, qualification and activities suitable for company's growth against 13.26% who thought it to be favoured by organisational rules, regulations and work environment. A *(b)* small number of respondents 7.14% explained that there is no such mechanism.

*(c)* To what extent workplace constitution protects the rights of organisational citizens?

The findings indicated that 48.1% of the respondents perceived that the workplace constitution seemed to protect the right of the organisational citizens to some extent against 26.7% who thought it to be to great extent. A small number of respondents (8.1%) reported it to be to little extent. Interestingly, 17 per cent of the respondents can not say anything. The obtained mean score was 3.93, which further substantiates the interpretation.

*(d)* The employees of this organisation are more concerned for their rights than their responsibilities.

The responses obtained on the item denied the assumption that the employees of this organisation are more concerned for their rights than their responsibilities, as the obtained mean score was 2.74. Further, 40.7% of the respondents reported it to be false against 26.7% who hold it to be true. 16.3% of the respondents said it to be quite false against 10.4% of them reporting it to be quite true.

*(7)* ***Organisational Existentialism:*** The variable was examined with the help of a number of items measuring the different dimensions related to the existence of an organisation.

*(a)* ***Mission Statement:*** It was procured with the help of an open-ended item where the respondents had to write in the provided space about the company's mission statement. The obtained responses were content analyzed and the findings indicated that 31.62% of the respondents reported their company's mission to be stakeholder satisfaction. 31.68 per cent of respondents reported it to be satisfaction and success through values and quality. However, only 19.38% expressed it to become a

part of world class leading and friendly company. A negligible number of respondents (5.10%) indicated social responsibility to be the company's mission. 12.22 per cent of the respondents did not provide any response.

One can have a better understanding of the finding from Figure—10.

**Figure—10**
**Company's Mission Statement as Perceived by the Respondents**

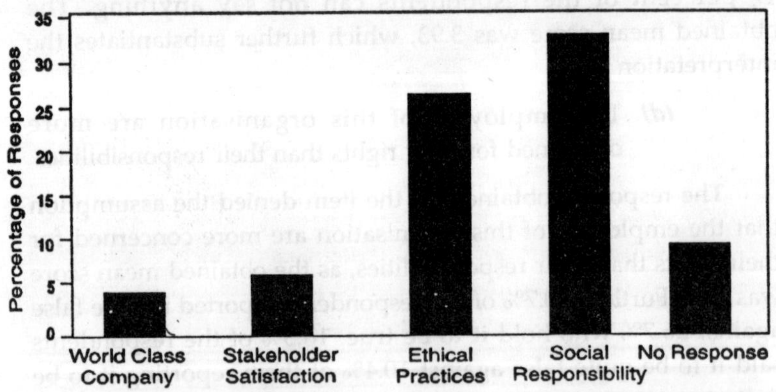


(b) *Guiding Principles:* The respondents were asked to comment on the guiding principles that their company followed. The findings showed that 47.95% of the respondents believed it to be maintaining values. 28.60 per cent of respondents reported the guiding principles of their company to promote community like work atmosphere. A very small percentage of respondents (4.08) reported it to create a learning community. 18.32 per cent of respondents did not provide any response. A negligible number of respondents (1.05%) stated it to be linking to society. Figure—11 better explains the results.

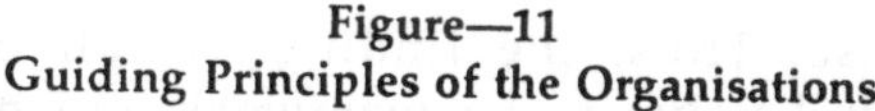

**Figure—11**
**Guiding Principles of the Organisations**

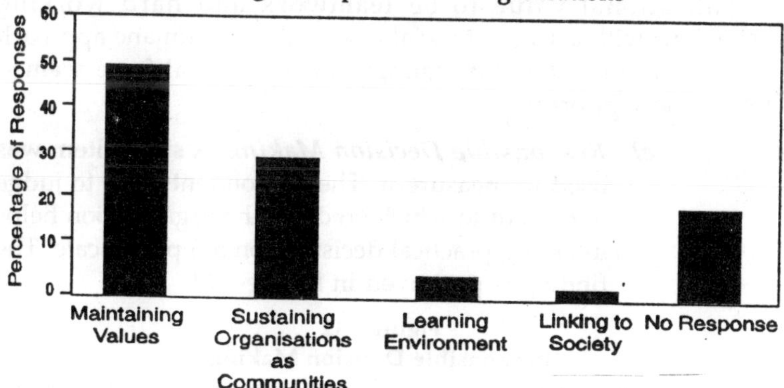


*(b)* ***Organisation Value/Credos:*** This was also open-ended item. The obtained responses were content analyzed and the percentage of response alongwith its categories are presented in Table—6.

**Table—6**
**Percentage of Response indicating the Organisational Values/Credos**

| *Organisational Values/Credos* | *Percentage of Responses* |
|---|---|
| 1. Fair practices | 31.62 |
| 2. Social responsibility | 19.38 |
| 3. Stakeholder satisfaction | 14.28 |
| 4. Community feeling | 11.26 |
| 5. Be a global force | 2.04 |
| 6. No response | 21.42 |

Note. N = 135.

Table—6 indicated fair practices to be the credos of the organisation as reported by 31.62% of the respondents. 14.28 percentage of said it to be stakeholder satisfaction. A good number of respondents indicated community feeling to be the value of the organisation (14.28%). Surprisingly, a negligible number of respondents (2.04) reported it to be a global force. The remaining percentage of respondents (21.42) did not provide any response. Thus, the finding overall indicated the organisational value to be teamwork and hard working behaviour with a sense of social responsibility, humane approach and ethical practices. Interestingly, to be a global force seemed to have low priority.

*(e) Responsible Decision Making:* A single item was used to measure it. The respondents had to judge the extent to which credo of the organisation helps in taking practical decisions on a 5-point scale. The finding is portrayed in Figure—12.

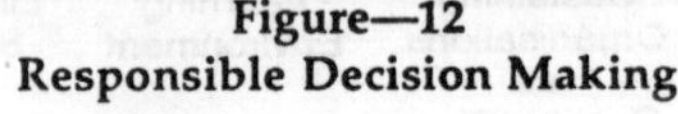

**Figure—12**
**Responsible Decision Making**

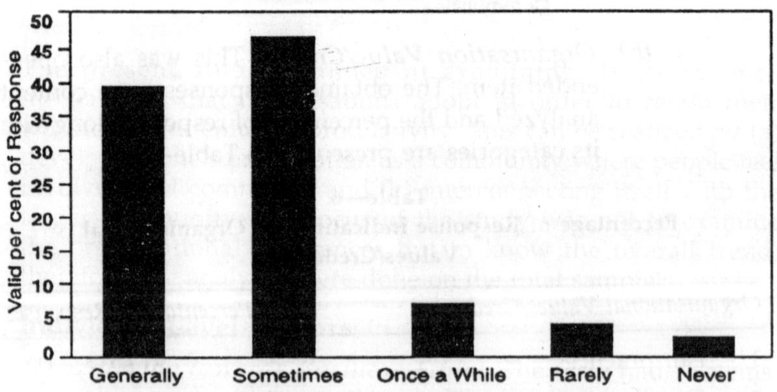


Figure—12 suggested that 47.4 per cent of the respondents reported that sometimes the credo of the organisation helps in taking practical decisions against 39.3% of them who said it be generally. The obtained mean score = 4.18 indicated it to be towards upper end, which provides support to the finding.

### *(8) Social Responsibility of the Organisations*

It was examined in two parts. In Part—I, an attempt was made to have a general understanding of the organisation's efforts towards connecting itself with the larger community. Part—II dealt with the specific activities related to organisation's responsiveness towards community.

## General Understanding

The examination on the issue started with an open-ended item stating,

**How do you connect yourself to the larger community?**

The obtained responses were content analyzed and entered in Table—7.

**Table—7**
**Percentage of Responses regarding the Way Organisations get connected to the Larger Community**

| | *Ways* | *percentage of Response* |
|---|---|---|
| 1. | Involve in social-welfare activities | 32.65 |
| 2. | Good customer service | 16.32 |
| 3. | Company is not concerned | 2.04 |
| 4. | Service to Nation | 14.28 |
| 5. | Environment protection efforts | 10.5 |
| 6. | No response | 24.48 |

Note. N = 135.

The procured percentage of responses as showed in Table—7 indicated that 32.65% of the respondents told it to be through social activities. 16.32 per cent of the respondents said it to be through good customer service. A small number of respondents (10.5%) expressed it to be through NGOs. 2.04 per cent of the respondents told that the company is not concerned. Some (14.28%) seemed to have very generalised perceptions, like being a part of the community and service to nation etc.

**Do you have any clear-cut stated policy on social development?**

58.5% of the respondents agreed that their oganisations don't have any clear-out policy on social development against 41.5% who thought it other way.

**What do you consider your social responsibility to be?**

- Towards employees
- Towards developing community
- Both

The findings disclosed that 31.1% of the respondents considered it to be towards employees, 36.3% viewed it to be towards developing community and 32.6 % of the respondents perceived the social responsibility of their organisation to be towards both.

**Do you adopt any village or community in order to develop?**

59.3 per cent of the respondents said no whereas 40.7 per cent of them accepted it. The difference in the finding may be because of two different types of organisations.

**What do you do to uplift the less privileged section of the society?**

This was an open-ended item. The content analyses of the obtained responses are entered in Table—8.

**Table—8**

**Percentage of Responses indicating Organisation's Efforts for the Upliftment of the Less Privileged Section of the Society**

| | *Efforts* | *Percentage of Responses* |
|---|---|---|
| 1. | Business—NGO partnership | 33.66 |
| 2. | Ad-hoc arrangements | 3.06 |
| 3. | Implementation of government schemes | 23.4 |
| 4. | No response | 38.68 |

Note. N = 135

Table—8 indicated that 33.66% of the respondents were of the view that they helped the under privileged section of the society through NGOs by providing them donations etc. 23.4% said by implementing government schemes. 3.06% of the respondents reported to have ad hoc arrangements in the organisation for such social activities. A larger chunk of the respondents (38.68%) were not able to provide any sort of responses. Thus, the finding clearly indicated that business social partnership is still not being focussed.

**Do you feel that giving donation to community for its development enhances the image of the company in the eyes of peers and of investing public?**

Only 43 per cent of the respondents responded in an affirmative fashion. 57 per cent of the respondents denied it.

**When you invest in social development, do you look at what is in it for you tomorrow or in the long term?**

The results disclosed that 24.4% of the respondents reported it to be generally a case, 25.95% were of opinion that it seemed to be true sometimes. The two together accounts 50.3% of respondents' views. 19.3 per cent held the view that it is rarely true against 10.4 per cent who report it to be never true. The reported mean score is 3.35 on a 5-point scale which again provides support to the fact that to some extent the statement stands true. Thus, no clear-cut trend emerged out of this.

**The company gives donation basically for image building and tax benefits.**

The reported mean score = 3.16 on a 5-point scale suggested that companies do not necessarily give donation for image building and tax benefit. 25.9% of the respondents strongly denied the fact. 8.9 per cent told it to be the case once a while 23.7 per cent reported it to be sometimes the case against that of 26.7% who believed it be always.

***Business Social Partnership:*** The responses were obtained in open-ended style to understand the business-social partnership in terms of:

(1) Nature of arrangements;

(2) Kind of activities initiated and;

(3 Responsibility for the attainment of communities goals.

***(1) Nature of arrangements:*** The responses were obtained on the arrangements made between organisation and those committed for community development (NGO) as an effort to examine business-social partnership. The majority of the respondents 68.3% did not respond to it. This clearly shows the absence of such an arrangement. Only 11.22% of the respondents expressed the views by being connected with NGO and 15.38% of respondents told by providing help to the target group directly through the company. A small number of respondents (5.10%) reported such arrangements not to be known to them.

(2) ***Kind of activities initiated:*** The obtained responses indicated that 17.42 per cent of the respondents reported it to be development related, i.e. organising welfare programmes, social functions, connected to NGOs, provide medical help etc. A very small number of respondents (9.18%) reported the initiativeness taken by the organisation towards environment related issues. A good number of respondents (30.6%) expressed the things not known to them. 42.8 per cent of the respondents did not provide any feedback on the issue. This clearly indicates the absence of a well established strategy to promote business-social partnership in organisations.

(3) ***Who is responsible for the attainment of community goals?*** The majority of the respondents (72.4%) have not written any thing. 5.16 per cent of the respondents reported the things not known to them. On the one hand 8.16 per cent of respondents were of the view that the administrative people are responsible for the attainment of community goals whereas on the other hand 7.14 per cent of respondents felt the whole team (i.e., NGO, company people and community members) to be responsible for it. A small number of respondents expressed the responsibility to lie with the NGOs (3.06%) and all members of the society (4.08%).

## Specific Activities

The organisation's responsiveness towards community were examined with specific reference to: (a) Purpose, (b) Motive, (c) Strategy, (d) Staff, (e) Structure, (f) Initiative, (g) Contribution, (h) Drivers and (i) Sustainability.

The findings (Appendix—II) indicated that 60% of the respondents were found to report healthy business environment as *the main purpose* of social responsibility. The *motive* behind such social activities was highlighted to be morality (by 55.6% of respondents) and long-term self-interest (by 34.1% of respondents.) About 44.4% of the respondents reported the *strategy* behind meeting such social responsibilities to be systematic. 57.9% of the respondents reported *all levels of management* to be involved in it and thus the *structure* of such activities seemed to be integrated with business functions (as highlighted by 48.2% of the respondents). Meeting social responsibilities by the organisations seemed to be based on initiating (33.3%) and integrated into daily decision making (25.9%). A good number of respondents (35.6%) explained the *initiatives* to be in the form of response to the requests in target areas. On the dimension of *contribution* made by the organisation for social development activities, no clear-cut trend emerged. It seemed to be a mixture of different kinds of contribution. 31.2% of respondents reported it to be in terms of cash and donations, skills and cash; 42.9% of them (respondents) explained the contribution to be in terms of business resources and 25.9% suggested it to be imbedded in profit and growth goals. An interesting finding emerged with respect to the *drivers* behind such social activities. Some said it to be chairman's whim (20% of the respondents), some perceived it to be a part of business strategy (31.1%), for some (27.4%) it seemed to be guidelines in place and for some (21.5%) it seemed to be business-linked guidelines in place. Finally, they were asked to judge the *sustainability* of such social activities. 59.3 per cent of the respondents reported it to be ongoing part of business management, goals and appraisals. It definitely seemed not to be, one offs as it was highlighted by only 2.2 per cent of the respondents. The point to be focussed is poor attention on nurturing NGOs and building their capacity (15.6 per cent) in order to establish business-social partnership for sustainable social activities.

### *(9) Business Strategies*

It was assumed that a good strategy leads to sustainable competitive advantage. Therefore, efforts were made to understand:

*(a)* What should be criteria for weeding out candidate strategies?

*(b)* How can a manager judge which strategic option is best for the company?

*(c)* What are the standards for determining whether a strategy is successful or not?

(a) ***Criteria for weeding out candidate strategies:*** The obtained views were content analysed. The pattern of responses indicated that while weeding out candidate strategies the managers seemed to give maximum importance to past experience (as reported by 29.5% of the respondents). 26.6% reported the selection of strategy to be after evaluating all strategies. Further, a small number of respondents (3.06%) attached importance to human values and its impact on the larger community before weeding out the candidate strategies. Quite a large number of respondents (40.78%) provided no response in this regard.

(b) ***Deciding strategic option best for the company:*** The content analyses of the obtained responses suggested that while deciding the best strategy to be adopted by the company the managers (as reported by 47.90% of respondents) seemed to do the cost-benefit evaluation of the strategies before selecting the final one. 18.38% of respondents hinted concern for human values to be the deciding factor while selecting the best strategy. A small number (12.30%) of respondents indicated past experience to be the determining factor in selecting the best strategic option for the company. Surprisingly, only 3.06% per cent of the respondents reported experimentation and intuition to be the base of strategy selection. The remaining percentage (18.36%) provided no response in this connection.

(c) ***Standards for determining a successful strategy:*** The obtained opinions were put for content analyses. The finding indicated that majority of the respondents (62.31%) felt effective results and success to be the standards for measuring whether a strategy is successful or not. 21.44 per cent of them (respondents) reported stakeholder satisfaction to be the standard for evaluating the success of any strategy. Only 2.04 per cent of the respondents said the ethical implications to be the determining factor for the success of a strategy. No response was obtained from 14.21 per cent of the respondents who participated in the study.

## (4) Suppliers

***Objective:*** To supply quality product at reasonable price on time was perceived by the majority (48.9%) of the respondents to be the objective of organisation's policy with respect to suppliers. 20.56 per cent expressed it to be professional. Loyal relationship and long-term relation was reported by 4.08 and 6.06 per cent of the respondents, respectively. A good number of respondents (20.4%) did not provide any response.

***Relationship:*** The content analyses of the responses disclosed that 32.82 per cent of the respondents believed the relationship between organisation and suppliers to be professional. 29.5 per cent reported the relationship to be cordial. A very small number (5.10%) of them (respondents) expressed the relationship to be as business-partners. Similarly, 4.08 per cent of respondents told the relationship to be long-term. No response was obtained by 28.5 per cent of the respondents.

## (5) Communities

***Objective:*** The objective of the organisation's policy to satisfy the expectations of the community was reported by 26.7 per cent of the respondents to be through good citizenship behaviour. Interestingly, 43.78 per cent of respondents thought it to be social welfare. A very small percentage of respondents' (6.12%) said the objective to be the mutual benefit of both, organisation as well as community. No response was obtained by 23.4 per cent of respondents.

***Relationship:*** The respondents (42%) said about the organisation's policy to maintain the relationship with the community in order to satisfy their expectations to be friendly. The majority (31.58%) did not provide any response. 16.32 per cent of the respondents perceived it to be by being a part of the society. A negligible number of respondents (5.1%) reported the organisation's policy to maintain the relationship with the community by being responsible towards the society. The partnership between community and organisation (as a matter of organisation's policy to maintain relationship) was highlighted by only 3.06 per cent of the respondents. 31.58 per cent of the respondents did not provide any response.

# Chapter—4

# DISCUSSION AND CONCLUSION

*"Business is not separate from society ... companies are not only engines of economic growth but also pivotal agents of social and political integration (Fombrun, 1998, p. 28).*

In this era of globalization when the consistent pressure on the organisations are, how to compete globally it becomes important to review the socio-cultural context in which the organisations are functioning. The question arises, what shall be the strategy of the organisations which functions in a developing country like India? Less openness, strong regulations on industry, slower rates of change and technological advance generally characterize the organisations in developing countries.

The author is of the view that to maintain sustainable competitive advantage the organisations need to do two main things:

(1) Position itself in the society and

(2) Tap the potential and commitment if its people.

This seems to be the deviation from traditional management practices. The new paradigms require a conscious business movement in which the organisation for its survival focuses on its social as well as cultural competence. This can be realized when the efforts are directed towards creating a community culture within the organisation. Consequently, the goal of the organisation, that, becomes something more than profit maximization. This leads the way for the organisations to be externally focussed which in return enhances its reputation in the eyes of the public.

But, immediately, the question comes to one's mind, can the organisations whose primary goals are to meet business obligations afford the costs of meeting its societal obligations. Probably, the answer is yes.

***Organisations, like individuals, have its self concept:*** This self-concept is the identity of the organisations. The economic identity of the organisation is its *realized self* and the social identity its *perceived self*. For sustainable competitive advantage it is important that both the selves function in synergy. This paves the way towards a holistic thinking about the role of organisations in to-day and tomorrow's society. This requires a good combination of pragmatic and reflective approach. The pragmatic approach will enable it to realize its business obligations and the reflective approach will help in establishing its credibility in the society. It has been empirically proved that responsible corporate behaviour can be in the best-economic interest of the stakeholders. The long run success of business depends on its ability to understand that it is a part of a larger society and to behave accordingly. If this is the case, then there is a need to understand the role of organisations against its socio-cultural context.

But before discussing it we need to address the question:

**Do the organisations exist only for profit?**

Let us start with a very simple definition of organisation. Can we describe organisation as a force field made up of the relationship among the people who associate with each other under a common banner? Without people the organisation is like a disbanded army. The organisation cannot imagine anything, cannot create anything, cannot sell anything, only the individuals who make up the organisations can do these things. Therefore, it becomes important to develop an 'understanding community" in which the focus seem to be to serve the needs of its stakeholders. The organisation remains a tool to create for the founders and their colleagues what they really want (Wealth, status, and joy in the work itself). But to do so it must also succeed as serving entity (Yales and Dais, 2001).

Bowen (1953) claimed the businesses have the obligation to "pursue those policies, to make those decisions, or to follow those lines of action which are desirable in terms of the objectives and values of our society" (p. 6). This suggests that corporate activities have to conform to established social norms and values.

The present study was an effort to understand organisations as communities, which includes both, its economic identity as well as social identity. The author proceeded with two lines of investigations:

1. How do organisations position itself in the society? And
2. How can the organisations tap the commitment and potential of its employees?

The two together gives a firm the sustainable competitive advantage. The findings of the study showed that organisations have well thought strategies to do business. It adopts a very pragmatic approach while deciding its business strategies. The businesses are market-driven and the results of the present study provided sufficient support for this. However, the study showed clear indications for new set of values, as the respondents perceived the mission statement of the company to be stakeholder satisfaction through values and quality; guiding principle to be maintaining values and credos of the organisation to be fair practices and community feeling. This clearly highlights that today business implies a focus that is embedded in the society and therefore the people, in and around organisation, influence it.

By providing a more open learning environment inside the organisation and by focusing on its organisational citizenship behaviour the organisations can be able to develop its social identity and competence. Such social competence is likely to facilitate its professional competence because it provides greater sense of psychological wellbeing to the employees. Such practices may not be felt as barriers in the way of competition and profitability rather it encourages it. The findings of the study disclosed that when the managers seemed to emphasize on competitiveness and profitability the employees seemed to contribute most in terms of suggesting ideas and those ideas being experimented. The employees were found to take the initiatives and those initiatives were valued. As a result they were found to develop multi-skills. Contrarily, when the managers seemed to believe in maximizing benefits there were less likely chances of suggesting ideas. Interestingly, the present study reported that when the attitude towards business seemed to focus on fair practices the managers were found to be able to tap the potential and commitment of the people it terms of suggesting ideas and developing multi-skills. Further, greater the belief in the fair practices in the organisations higher was the stakeholder satisfaction and involvement.

The emphasis on competition and profitability along with fair practices helped the organisation to take rational decisions and to initiate social activities, which they planned in long-term perspective. Isabelle Maignan too reports almost similar findings (1999). On the contrary, when the organisation holds a purely economic attitude towards business—Business world has its own rules—it seemed to give donations basically for image building and tax benefits.

Therefore, the attitude that one holds towards business is greatly influenced by one's socio-cultural context. This is a deviation from the conventional approaches. The issue worth mentioning becomes how to establish a link between the important agents responsible for the nations socio-economic development. Prior to that, the questions that need to be addressed at this point are:

(1) Is the business only maximising profit? Or

(2) Do the organisations have some societal commitments?

(3) Should the business strategy incorporate only customer satisfaction and shareholder value or recognize broader social obligations?

The author advocates the organisational existentialism approach. This incorporates organisation's responsibilities and duties towards both; the internal community, which comprises people who work there and the larger community where it is located.

The benefits of high-integrity and high-responsibility organisations are well established conscience mechanisms that emphasize on fair practice which are manifested in responsible decision making and organisational citizenship behaviour. This cannot be possible unless and until the organisation combines a reflective approach in its managerial style. The reflective managerial style on the one hand provides caring climate to the organisation where members freely interact and have a free frank dialogue and on the other hand is aware of the purpose of its existence in the society.

The findings with respect to the former assumption showed that though the employees seemed to suggest ideas but their ideas were not being tried out to a considerable extent. There was not enough encouragement for people to contribute to organisational success. The people on the other hand felt that there is not much scope to develop multiple skills but the initiative was found to be valued. The trend indicates that much need to be done in order to make the workplace a learning community where members are encouraged to learn and contribute for the sake of organisational as well as personal development.

The organisations ask for the total commitment of the employees and in return provide challenging and interesting opportunities to the employees (as reported by the study). Therefore initiatives taken by the employees for collective enterprise were given importance. However, concern for collective enterprise needs to be given more weightage in order to mobilize the collective efforts of the employees, which can only happen when the organisation is a transparent community.

Transparency in the organisation can be perceived when it has fair practices and high standards of business ethics, which is manifested in its day-to-day dealings. Auditing of the business environmental ethical social and profitability bottom lines will enable the business to make a difference to the continuous improvement of the organisation. And in doing that, to make continuous improvement to overall society (Birch, 2000). To do this the organisations should be very clear about its own intentions towards various stakeholders. The findings indicated that in the sampled organisations, the company's mission statement was 'satisfaction and success through value based practices and quality work'. Managers seemed to believe in fair practices as guiding principles and therefore the credos of the organisations were reported to be fair practices along with stakeholder satisfaction. But the reality indicated (based on results) that stakeholders satisfaction and involvement was only up to some extent. Further, the responsible decision making seemed not to be integrated into managerial decision making practices. At this point it can be said that there is need for sustaining organisations as communities which is both *transparent* and *learning* for maintaining sustainable competitive advantage.

The results hinted towards a poor business-social partnership. However, the organisation's responsiveness towards community was perceived to be aimed at healthy business environment with a motive of morality and long-term self-interest. The company's initiatives in social domain seemed to be based on the request of the target group. The sustainability was reported to be an ongoing concern of business goals. Still in the absence of a clear-cut policy on social development the companies seemed to have poor business-social partnership.

Traditionally business viewed the social sector as a dumping ground for spare cash, obsolete equipment, and tired executives. But today smart companies are approaching it as a learning laboratory. Today, several leading companies are beginning to find inspiration in an unexpected place—the social sector—in public schools, welfare—to work programmes, and the inner city. These companies have discovered that social problems are economic problems, whether it is the need for a trained workforce or the search for new markets in neglected parts of cities.

They have learned that applying their energies to solving the chronic problems of the social sector powerfully stimulates their own business development. Today's better-educated children are tomorrow's knowledge workers. Lower unemployment in the inner city means higher consumption in the inner city. Indeed a new paradigm for innovation is emerging a partnership between private enterprise and public interest that produces profitable and sustainable changes for both sides. This requires a serious cultural change in the corporate world, which need to be understood by government and community. This change is designed to increase the rewards for all, including financial profit (Birch, 2000).

Kanter (1999) argues persuasively for the value of such business/community partnership and suggests six main characteristics of successful private/public partnerships: (1) a clear business agenda, (2) strong partners committed to change, (3) investment by both parties, (4) rootedness in the user community (5) links to other community organisations and (6) a long term commitment to sustain and replicate the results. The best way to ensure full commitment is to have both partners put their resources on the line (p. 128)

## Implication of the Research

The present study was an effort to understand how do the organisations maintain the competitive advantage. It was assumed that it could be achieved only when the organisation incorporates organisations performs in organisational citizenship behaviour, which can be realized in two ways: (1) developing one's organisation as a community where people feel involved and committed and (b) interconnecting itself with the larger community. The findings clearly indicated that this pursuit couldn't be realized unless and until the organisations have a well-established conscience mechanism. The results indicated the absence of such a mechanism. The findings of the study clearly implied that in order to sustain the competitive advantage we have to have a strategic approach that focus on economic growth along with social cohesion. The objective of business is not only to make profit but also to retain the talented people by providing a learning community and be a good corporate citizen by responding to the societal needs.

The new paradigms of partnership need to be developed and favoured which, of course is something more than corporate philanthropy. The new partnership, which will be between government, business and society, need to be based on social commitment of the organisation. The author advocated applying community development techniques in the organisations in order to transform it into a community.

happen". Such leaders need to be identified and supported fully which will help in changing the workplace atmosphere completely—a perfect feeling of community.

4. ***Learn how to host good gatherings:*** To convert the organisation atmosphere in to a community feeling it is necessary that the builder should have certain skills of hosting great conversations and designing gatherings which should be different from the traditional skills of good organisational meeting management. The necessary requirements for good gatherings are: meeting sites should be relaxing, food available as often as possible rather than having periodically, decisions to be recorded and the focussed points clear to everyone, group should be encouraged to take the responsibility of deciding the next agenda, pin point the people who can contribute, get volunteers and finally the sharing of 'learnings' and 'yearnings'. What the group has learnt from this get together and what need to be improved in the next get together.

5. ***Acknowledge the people's contribution:*** Acknowledgement is one of the most fundamental tools of community building. Everyone who contributes should be thanked and honoured for what they have done.

6. ***Involve the whole person:*** Use of music, art, symbols and drama should be encouraged to tap the deeper sources of knowing and intuition. For example, in one mass visioning and strategy effort, a large hot balloon floated outside the plan to symbolize the importance of a larger perspective.

7. ***Celebrate:*** What is the point of building community if we can not have fun? Community development work has to engage people's hearts, minds, spirits, and bodies. A key vehicle for this is celebration. Celebrate and recognize success, even if it is small. Celebrations do not cost lots of money. The only requirement is imagination.

## REFERENCES

Agarwal, K.G. (1976). Self, role and status: Towards satisfaction theory of work motivation. New Delhi: National Labour Institute.

Akers, J. F. (1989) Ethics and competitiveness *Sloan Management Review, 30* (2), pp. 69-72.

Albert, S. & Whetten, D.A. (1985). Managing the dual identity organisation. *Paper Presented at the Annual Meeting of the Academy of Management*, Vancouver, Canada.

Aram, J. (1989). The paradox of interdependent relations in the field of social issues in Management. *Academy of Management Review, 14*, pp. 266-283.

Arrow, K. J. (1974). Social responsibility and economic efficiency. *Public Policy, 21*, pp 303-317.

Ashforth, B.E. & Mael, F.A. (1996) Organisational identity and strategy as a context for the individual *Advances in Strategic Management* 13, pp. 17-62. Greenwich, CT: JAI Press.

Aupperle, K. Carroll, A & Hattfield, J. (1985). An empirical examination of the Relationship betwen corporate social responsibility and profitability. *Academy of Management Journal, 28* (2), pp. 446-463.

Barney, J. (1991). Firm resources and sustained competitive advantage. *Journal of Management 17* (1), pp. 99-120.

Baucus, M. & Nea, J. (1991). Can illegal corporate behaviour be predicted? An event history analysis. *Academy of Management Journal, 34* (1), pp. 9-36.

Bearle, A & Means, G. (1934). The modern corporation and private property. New York: Mac Millan.

Birch, D. (2000). Business as a public culture: Some principles of corporate citizenship. *Paper presented in International Roundtable Conference on "Corporate Reputation and Competitive Advantage." February 23-26, 2000; Human Values Centre, Indian Institute of Management Calcutta.*

Blumberg, D.A. (1987) Developing service as a line of business *Management Review, 76*, pp. 58-62.

Blume, E.R. (1987). Customer service: Giving customers the competitive edge. *Training Development Journal*, pp. 24-31.

Burke, K. (1937). Attitudes towards history. New York: New Republic.

Burke, L & Logdson, J. M. (1996). How corporate social responsibility pays off. *Long Range Planning, 29* (4), pp. 495-502.

Business Week (1995). Blind ambition: How the pursuit of results got out of hand at Bausch & Lomb. October 23, pp. 78-90.

Carroll, A. B. (1979). A three-dimensional conceptual model of corporate performance. *Academy of Management Review, 4* (4), pp. 497-505.

Chattopadhyay, G.P. (1975). Dependence in Indian culture. From mud huts to company Board rooms. *Economic and Political Weekly, 10,* pp. M30-M38.

Chattopadhyay, S.N. & Rao, T.V. (1970). Aspirations and apprehensions of small Industry personnel and their relationship with apparent Productivity. *Indian Journal of Psychology, 45,* pp. 39-52.

Chen, A.Y.S., Sawyers, R.B. & Williams, P.E. (1977). Reinforcing ethical decision Making through corporate culture. *Journal of Business Ethics, 16,* pp. 055-065.

Cheney, G. (1991). Rhetoric in an organisational society: managing multiple identities. Columbia: University of South Carolina Press.

Coleman, J.S. (1992). The rational reconstruction of society. *American Sociological Review, 58,* pp. 1-15.

Cyert, R. & March, J. (1963). A behavioural theory of the firm. Englewood Cliffs: Prentice-Hall.

Davis, K. (1973). The case for and against business assumptions of social responsibilities. *Academy of Management Journal, 16* (2), pp. 312-322.

Davies, P.W.F. (1992). The contribution of the philosophy of technology to the Management of technology. Ph.D thesis, Brunel University with Henley Management College.

Day, G.S. (1994). Continuous learning about markets. *California Management Review,* (Summer), pp. 9-31.

Dayal, I. (1976). Cultural factors in designing performance appraisal system, New Delhi: SRC, Industrial Relations and Human Resources.

De, N. (1974). Conditions for work culture. *Indian Journal of Industrial Relations, 9,* pp. 587-598.

Demsetz, H. (1995). First commentary—the firm in theory: Its definition and existence. In H. Demsetz (ed.). The Economics of Business Firm: Seven Critical Commentaries (pp. 1-14). Cambridge, England: Cambridge University Press.

Dill, W. (1975). Public participation in corporate planning: Strategic management in Kibitzer's world *Long Range Planning,* pp. 57-63.

Dorfman, P. (1988). Dimensions of national culture and effective leadership patterns: Hofstede revisited. *Advances in International Comparative Management, 3*, pp. 127-150.

Feldman, S.D. (1979). Nested identities. In N.K. Denzin (ed.) *Studies in Symbolic Interaction* (vol. 2, pp. 399-418). Greenwich, CT: JAI Press.

Fomburn, C.J. (1998). Three pillars of corporate citizenship: Ethics, social benefit, Profitability. In Noel Tichy et al (eds.) *Corporate Global Citizenship: doing Business in the Public Eye* (pp. 27-42). San Francisco: The New Lexington Press.

Ford, R. & Mc Laughlin, F (1984). Perceptions of socially responsible activities and Attitudes: A comparision of business deans corporate chief executives. *Academy of Management Journal*, 27, pp. 656-674.

Foreman, P & Whetten, D.A. (1997). An identity theory perspective on multiple Expectations in organisations. Working Paper, University of Illinois at Urbana Campaign.

Freeman, E. & Reed, D. (1983). Stockholders and stakeholders: A new perspective on corporate governance. *California Management Review, 15* (3), pp. 88-106.

Freeman, R. (1984). Strategic Management: A stakeholder approach. Boston: Pitman/Ballinger (Harper Collins).

Freidman, M. (1970). The social responsibility of business is to increase its profits. *New York Times Magazine*, September 13, p. 32.

Frez, M. & Early, P.C. (1993). Culture, self-identity and work. Oxford: Oxford University Press.

Ganesh, S.R. & Malhotra, A.K. (1975). Work values of Indian managers. *ASCI Journal of Management, 4* (2), pp. 147-162.

Galbraith, J. (1972) The new industrial state. 2nd edition. Boston: Houghton Mafflin.

Gehani, R.R. (1993). Quality value-chain: A meta-synthesis of frontiers of quality movement. *The Academy of Management Executive, 7* (2), pp. 29–42.

Giddens, A. (1984). The constitution of society. Berkley: University of California Press.

Golden-Biddle, K. & Rao, H. (1997). Breaches in the boardroom: Organisational identity And conflict of commitment in a non-profit organisation. *Organisation Science, 8* pp. 593-611.

Goyder, G. (1993). The just enterprise London: Adamantine Press.

Hamel, G. & Prahalad, C.K. (1989). Strategic intent. *Harvard Business Review, 67*, pp. 63-76.

Hartline, M.D. and Ferrell, O. C. (1996). The management of customer-contact service Employees: An empirical investigation. *Journal of Marketing, 60*, pp. 52-70.

Hesket, J.L., Sasser Jr. W.E. and Schlesinger, L.A. (1997). The service profit chain. New York: The Free Press.

Hofstede, G. (1980). Culture's consequences: International differences in work — related Values. Newbury Park, CA: Sage.

Hofstede, G. (1991). Cultures and orgaisations: Software of the mind. London: McGraw Hill.

Hopkins, M. (1999). Corporate social responsibility around the world. *On Line Journal*.

Jacobson, R. and Aaker, D.A. (1987). The strategic role of product quality. *Journal of Marketing, 51* pp. 31-44.

James Jr. H.S. (2000). Reinforcing ethical decision making through organisational structure. *Journal of Business Ethics, 28* (1), pp. 43-58.

James, W. (1890). Principles of psychology. Vol. 1 & 2. New York: Holt.

Jha, H. (1997). Role of voluntary organisation (NGO) in the rural development: Understanding the conditions of "empowerment". *The Social Engineer, 6* (1), pp. 37-38.

Jones, T. (1995). Instrumental stakeholder theory: A synthesis of ethics and economics. *Academy of Management Review, 20* (4), pp. 404-439.

Jonker, J. (2000). Organisations as responsible contributors to society: Linking quality. Sustainability and accountability. *Total Quality Management, 11* (4-6), pp. 741-746.

Kahle, D. (2000). Teaching your organisation to learn. *Agency Sales, 30* (9), pp. 61-64.

Kakar, S. (1978). The inner world: A psycho-analytic study of childhood and society in India. New Delhi: Oxford University Press.

Kanter, R.S. (1999). From spare charge to real change. The social sector as a Beta site for business innovation. *Harvard Business Review*, May/June Issue, pp. 122-32.

Kluckholm, F. (1954). Culture and behaviour. New York: Free Press.

Korduupleski, R.E. Rust, R.T. and Zahork, A.J. (1993). Why improved quality doesn't improve quality (Or whatever happened to marketing). *California Management Review, 35*, pp. 82-95.

Kothari, R. (1970). Politics in India, New Delhi: Orient Longman.

Kraft, K. and Hage, J. (1989). Strategy, social responsibility and implementation. *Journal of Business Ethics, 9* (1), pp. 11-19.

Kramer, R.M. (1993). Co-operation and organisational identification. In J.K. Murnighan (ed.). Social Psychology in Organisations: Advances in Theory and Research (pp. 244-268). Englewood Cliffs, NJ: Prentice-Hall.

Krep, D.M. (1990). Corporate culture and economic theory. In James Alt and Kenneth Shepsle (eds.), *Perspective on Positive Political Economy*. New York: Cambridge University Press.

Loe, T.W. (1996) The role of the ethical climate in developing trust, market orientation, and Commitment to quality. Unpublished Dissertation. The University of Memphis.

Maignan, I. (2000). Measuring corporate citizenship in two countries: The case of the United States and France. *Journal of Business Ethics, 23* (3), pp. 283-297.

Markus, H &Nurius, P. (1986). Possible selves. *American Psychologists, 41*, pp. 954-969.

Marriot, K. (1977). Changing identities in South-Asia. In K.A. David (ed.) *The new wind: Changing identities in South-Asia*. The Hague, Paris, Mouton, Chicago, Aldine.

McCall, G.J. & Simmons, J.L. (1978). Identities and interactions: An examination of Associations in everyday life (revised ed.). New York.

McGuire, J., Sundgren, A. Schneeweis, T. (1988). Corporate social responsibility and firm financial performance. *Academy of Management Journal, 31* (4), pp. 854-872.

McIntosh, M. Leipziger, D. Jones, B. & Coleman, J. (1998). Corporate citizenship; Successful strategies for responsible companies. *Financial Time Management*, London.

Mead, G.H. (1934). Mind, self and society. Chicago; University of Chicago Press.

Mehta, V. (1998). A long-term strategy. *Business World*, February 22nd Issue, pp. 86-88.

Moran, P. & Ghoshal, S. (1999). Markets, firms and the process of economic development. Academy of Management. *The Academy of Management Review, 24*, pp. 390-412.

Mullen, J. (1997). Performance-based corporate philanthropy: How 'giving smart' can further corporate goals. *Public Relations Quarterly*, (Summer), pp. 42-48.

Neal, C. (1999). A conscious change in the workplace. *The Journal for Quality and Participation*, 22 (2), pp. 27-30.

Nonaka, I. (1991). The knowledge creating company. *Harvard Business Review, 69* (6), pp. 96-104.

Palazzi, M. & Starcher, G. (2001). Corporate social responsibility and business success. *http://www.ebbf.org/crswrd.html*

Phillips, L.W., Chang, D.R. And Buzzell (1983). Product quality, cost position and business performance: A test of some key hypotheses. *Journal of Marketing, 47*, pp. 26-43.

Porter, M.E. (1985). Competitive advantage: Creating and Sustaining Superior Performance. New York: The Free Press.

Prahalad, C.K. & Hamel, G. (1990). The core competence of the corporation. *Harvard Business Review, 68*, pp. 79-91.

Pratt, M.G. & Rafaeli, A. (1997). Organisational dress as a symbol of multilayered social identities. *Academy of Management Journal, 40* pp. 862-898.

Preston, L. & Post, J. (1975). Private management and public policy: The principle of public responsibility. Englewood Cliffs: Prentice-Hall.

Preston. L.E. & 'O' Bannon, D.P. (1978). Analyzing corporate social performance: Methods and results. *Journal of Contemporary Business*, 7, p. 135-149.

Reger, R.K. Barney, J. Bunderson, S., Foreman, P., Gustafson, L.T., Huff, A.S. Martens, L., Sarason, Y & Stimpert, L. (1998). A strategy conversation on the topic of organisational identity. In D. Whetten & P. Godfrey (eds). *Identity in Organisations: Developing Theory through Conversations* (pp. 99-168). Thousand Oaks, CA: Sage.

Reichel, A. and Neumann (1988). Attitude towards business ethics questionnaire, *Journal of Instructional Psychology*, March Issue, pp. 25-33.

Roland, A. (1980). The self in India and America. In V. Kavolis (ed.) *In Designs of Selfhood* (pp. 170-191). New Jersey: Associated University Press.

Scott, S. G. & Lane, V.R. (2000). A stakeholder approach to organisational identity. *Academy of Management Review*, 25(1), pp. 43-62.

Seth, Meera (1998). Profit and philanthropy. *Business World*. February 22nd Issue, pp. 80-83.

Senge, Peter (1992). The fifth discipline, Britain: Banton Doubleday Dell Publishing Group.

Senge, P.M.; Kleiner, A.; Roberts, C.; Ross, R.B.; Smith, B.J. (1994). The fifth discipline Fieldbook: Strategies and tools for building a learning organisation. New York: Doubleday.

Shapiro, C. (1983). Premiums for high quality products as returns to Reputations. *Quarterly Journal of Economics, 98*, pp. 659-679.

Shweder, R.A. & Levine, R.A. (1984). Culture theory: Essays on mind, self and emotion. New York: Cambridge University Press.

Simon, H.A. (1991). Organisations and markets. Journal of Economic Perspectives, 5, pp. 25-44.

Singh-Sengupta, Sunita (1990). Emerging patterns of power distribution: A study of Banking organisations. New Delhi: Commonwealth Publisher.

Sinha, J.B.P. (1980). The nurturant task leader: A model of the effective executive. New Delhi: Concept Publishing House.

Sinha, J.B.P. (1970). Development through behaviour modification. Bombay: Allied.

Slater, S.F. & Narver, J.C. (1995). Market orientation and the learning organisation. *Journal of Marketing, 58*, pp. 162-167.

Smith, D.K. Paradice, D.B. & Smith, S.M. (2000). Prepare your mind for creativity. *Association for computing machinery: Communications of the ACM 43*, (7), pp. 110-116.

Sonnenberg, F.K. (1989). Service quality: Forethought not afterthought. *The Journal of Business Strategy*, pp. 54-57.

Stanwick, P.A. & Stanwick, S.D. (1998). The relationship between corporate social Performance and organisational size, financial performance and environmental performance: An empirical examination. *Journal of Business Ethics, 17*, pp. 195-204.

Stata, R. (1989). Organisational learning–The key to management innovation. *Sloan Management Review, 30* (3) pp. 63-74.

Stone, C. (1975). Where the law ends. New York: Harper & Row.

Stryker, S. & Serpe, R (1982). Commitment, identity salience and role behaviour: Theory and research example. In W. Ickers & E. Knowles (eds.). Personality, Roles and Social Behaviour (pp. 199-219). New York: Springer-Verlag.

Suchman, M.C. (1995). Managing legitimacy: Strategic and institutional approaches. *Academy of Management Journal, 20*, pp. 571-610.

Tajfel, H. & Turner, J.C. (1979). An integrative theory of intergroup conflict. In W.G. Austin & S. Worchel (eds.). The Social Psychology of Group Relations (pp. 33-47). Monterey, CA: Brooks-Cole.

Trevino, L.K., Butterfield, K.D. & McCabe, D.L. (1998). The ethical context in Organisations: Influences on employee attitudes and behaviours. *Business Ethics Quarterly, 8* (3), pp. 447-476.

Venkateswaran, S. (1998). Develop, don't donate. *Business World*, February 22nd Issue, pp. 83-86.

Venkat Ramani, S.H. http:/www.lifepositive.com/mind/ethics and values/ethics_article. html.

Victor, B. & Cullen, J.B. (1988). The organisational bases of ethical work climates. *Administrative Science Quarterly, 33,* pp. 101-125.

Watrick, S. & Cochran, P. (1985). The evolution of the corporate social performance model. *Academy of Management Review, 10,* pp. 758-769.

Wood, D. (1991). Corporate social performance revisited. *Academy of Management Review, 16* (4), pp. 691-718.

Zadek, S. Pruzan, P & Evans, R (1997). Building corporate accountability: Emerging practices in social and ethical accounting, auditing and reporting. London: Earthscan Publication.

Zithaml, V.A.; Berry, L.L. and Parasuraman (1988). Communication and control processes in the delivery of service quality. *Journal of Marketing, 52,* pp. 35-48.

# APPENDIX—I

## ATTITUDE TOWARDS BUSINESS ETHICS

**Maximising Benefits**

| | *Item Description* | *Factor Loading* |
|---|---|---|
| 1. | The only moral of business is making money. | .58 |
| 2. | A person who is doing well in business does not have to worry about moral problems. | .65 |
| 3. | Ethics in business is basically an adjustment. | .61 |
| 4. | Moral values are irrelevant to the business world. | .75 |
| 5. | "Business Ethics" is a concept for public relation only. | .68 |
| 6. | As a consumer, when making an auto insurance claim, I try to get as much as possible regardless of the extent of the damage. | .71 |
| 7. | While shopping at the super market it is appropriate to switch price tags on packages. | .63 |
| 8. | As an employee I can take office supplies, it does not hurt anyone. | .54 |
| 9. | I view sick days & vacation days that I deserve. | .49 |

*Note.* N = 135. *Eigen Value* = 4.26; *Percentage of Variance Explained* = 23.64.

### Emphasis on Competitiveness and Profitability

| | Item Description | Factor Loading |
|---|---|---|
| 1. | Competitiveness and profitability are important values. | .72 |
| 2. | Conditions for a free economy will best serve the needs of society. Limiting competition can only hurt society and actually violates basic natural laws. | .63 |
| 3. | If you want a specific goal, you have to take the necessary steps. | .51 |
| 4. | A good businessperson is a successful businessperson. | .53 |

*Note.* N = 135. *Eigen Value* = 2.62; Percentage of Variance Explained = 14.53.

### Fair Practices

| | Item Description | Factor Loading |
|---|---|---|
| 1. | Every businessperson acts according to moral principles, whether he or she is aware of it or not. | -.45 |
| 2. | Act according to the law, and you can't go wrong morally. | .42 |
| 3. | Employees wages should be determined according to the laws of supply and demand | .48 |

*Note.* N = 135. *Eigen Value* = 1.54; *Percentage of Variance Explained* = 8.54.

### Rational Decision

| | Item Description | Factor Loading |
|---|---|---|
| 1. | Business decisions involve a realistic economic attitude and not a moral philosophy. | -.52 |

*Note.* N = 135. *Eigen Value* = 1.39; *Percentage of Variance Explained* = 7.70.

## Business World has its own rules

| | *Item Description* | *Factor Loading* |
|---|---|---|
| 1. | The business world has its own rules. | .56 |

*Note.* N = 135. *Eigen Value* = 1.02; *Percentage of Variance Explained* = 5.69.

# APPENDIX—II

## PERCEPTION OF ORGANISATIONAL CULTURE

### Authoritative

| | *Item Description* | *Factor Loading* |
|---|---|---|
| 1. | Manager should not delegate difficult and important tasks to their subordinates. | .76 |
| 2. | It is more important for men to have a professional career than it is for women to have a professional career. | .78 |
| 3. | Women do not value recognition and promotion in their work as much as men do. | .78 |

*Not.* N = 135. *Eigen Value* = 4.50; *Percentage of Variance Explained* = 18.01.

### Power Orientation

| | *Item Description* | *Factor Loading* |
|---|---|---|
| 1. | Rules and regulations are important because they inform the worker what the organisation expects of them. | .69 |
| 2. | It is important for manager to encourage loyalty and a sense of duty to the group. | .78 |
| 3. | Manager should be careful not to ask the opinion of subordinates too frequently. | .39 |

Note. *N* = *135.* Eigen Value = *2.43;* Percentage of Variance Explained = *9.70*

## Normative Behaviour

| | *Item Description* | *Factor Loading* |
|---|---|---|
| 1. | It is important to have job requirements and instructions spelled out so people always know what they are expected to do. | .60 |
| 2. | Individual rewards are not as important as group welfare. | .62 |
| 3. | Group success is more important than individual success. | .55 |
| 4. | It is preferable to have a man in high-level position rather than a woman. | .47 |
| 5. | There are some jobs which a man can always do better than a woman. | .62 |

Note. *N = 135*. Eigen Value = *2.23;* Percentage of Variance Explained = *8.91*.

## Power Distance

| | *Item Description* | *Factor Loading* |
|---|---|---|
| 1. | Managers should take most decisions without consulting subordinates | .70 |
| 2. | It is often necessary for a superior to emphasize his or her authority and power when dealing with subordinates. | .71 |
| 3. | Subordinates should not disagree with their manager's decisions. | .50 |
| 4. | Meetings are usually run more effectively when they are chaired by a man. | .40 |

Note. *N = 135*. Eigen Value = *1.10;* Percentage of Variance Explained = *7.98*.

## Stereotyped Perception

| | *Item Description* | *Factor Loading* |
|---|---|---|
| 1. | An individual should not pursue his or her own objectives without considering the welfare of the group. | -.71 |
| 2. | Men usually solve problems with logical analysis, women usually solve problems with intuition. | .79 |
| 3. | Solving organisational problems usually requires the active forcible approach, which is typical of men. | .60 |

Note. *N* = *135*. Eigen Value = *1.50;* Percentage of Variance Explained = *6.01*.

## Job Clarity

| | *Item Description* | *Factor Loading* |
|---|---|---|
| 1. | Standard operating procedures are helpful to workers on the job. | .78 |
| 2. | Instructions for operations are important for workers on the job. | .81 |

Note. *N* = *135*. Eigen Value = *1.31;* Percentage of Variance Explained = *5.25*.

## Acceptance in Group

| | *Item Description* | *Factor Loading* |
|---|---|---|
| 1. | Being accepted by the group is more important than working on your own. | .90 |

Note. *N* = *135*. Eigen Value = *1.26;* Percentage of Variance Explained = *5.03*.

## Social Relationships

| | *Item Description* | *Factor Loading* |
|---|---|---|
| 1. | A manager should avoid socializing with his or her subordinates off the job. | .84 |
| 2. | Women are more concerned with social aspects of their job than they are with getting ahead | .55 |

Note. *N* = *135*. Eigen Value = *1.20;* Percentage of Variance Explained = *4.77*.

## Managerial Styles

| | *Item Description* | *Factor Loading* |
|---|---|---|
| 1. | Managers expect workers to closely follow instructions and procedures. | .58 |
| 2. | Women value working in a friendly atmosphere than men do. | .74 |

Note. *N. 135*. Eigen Value = *1.00;* Percentage of Variance Explained = *4.01*.

# APPENDIX—III

**The Valid Percentage of Responses on Orgaisation's Responsiveness towards Community**

| *Variables* | *Numerical Value* | *Valid Percentage of Responses* |
|---|---|---|
| 1. ***Purpose*** | | |
| (a) Philanthropy | 1 | 10.40 |
| (b) Strategic philanthropy | 2 | 17.0 |
| (c) Community investment | 3 | 12.6 |
| (d) Healthy business environment | 4 | 60.0 |
| **Mean Score = 3.18** | | |
| **SD Score = 1.78** | | |
| 2. ***Motive*** | | |
| (a) Morality | 1 | 55.6 |
| (b) Long-term self interest | 2 | 34.1 |
| (c) Long-term direct self interest | 3 | 5.9 |
| (d) Direct self interest | 4 | 4.4 |
| **Mean Score = 1.52** | | |
| **SD Score = 0.88** | | |

| | | |
|---|---|---|
| **3. *Strategy*** | | |
| (a) Adhoc | 1 | 21.5 |
| (b) Systematic | 2 | 44.4 |
| (c) Strategic | 3 | 23.0 |
| (d) Organisational ownership | 4 | 11.1 |
| **Mean Score = 2.20** | | |
| **SD Score = 0.98** | | |
| **4. *Staff*** | | |
| (a) Administrator | 1 | 22.9 |
| (b) Manager | 2 | 8.1 |
| (c) Entrepreneur/Consultant | 3 | 11.1 |
| (d) Integrated at all management levels | 4 | 57.9 |
| **Mean Score = 2.98** | | |
| **SD Score = 1.37** | | |
| **5. *Structure*** | | |
| (a) Detached from business activity | 1 | 27.4 |
| (b) Detached but linked in business interests | 2 | 20.0 |
| (c) Part of line structure | 3 | 4.4 |
| (d) Integrated with business functions | 4 | 48.2 |
| **Mean Score = 2.67** | | |
| **SD Score = 1.41** | | |

| | | |
|---|---|---|
| **6. *Initiative*** | | |
| (a) Passive | 1 | 5.2 |
| (b) Responsive to requests in target areas | 2 | 35.6 |
| (c) Initiating | 3 | 33.3 |
| (d) Integrated into daily decision making | 4 | 25.9 |
| **Mean Score = 2.67** | | |
| **SD Score = 1.12** | | |
| **7. *Contribution*** | | |
| (a) Mainly cash or goods | 1 | 10.5 |
| (b) Cash and donations, skills and cash | 2 | 20.7 |
| (c) Business resources | 3 | 42.9 |
| (d) Imbedded in profit and growth goals | 4 | 25.9 |
| **Mean Score = 2.67** | | |
| **SD Score = 1.15** | | |
| **8. *Drivers*** | | |
| (a) Chairman's whim | 1 | 20.0 |
| (b) Guidelines in place | 2 | 27.4 |
| (c) Business-linked guidelines in place | 3 | 21.5 |
| (d) Part of business strategy | 4 | 31.1 |
| **Mean Score = 2.58** | | |
| **SD Score = 1.23** | | |

| 9. *Sustainability* | | |
|---|---|---|
| (a) One offs | 1 | 2.2 |
| (b) Assistance on specific issues | 2 | 22.9 |
| (c) Nurturing NGOs and building their capacity | 3 | 15.6 |
| (d) Ongoing part of business management, goals and appraisals | 4 | 59.3 |
| **Means Score = 3.18** | | |
| **SD Score = 1.19** | | |

Note. N = 135

# Index